ASP.NET Core

"A Beginner's Guide to Efficient Web APIs with ASP.NET Core"

Clayton Fleming

© **Copyright 2023 - All rights reserved.**

The contents of this book may not be reproduced, duplicated or transmitted without direct written permission from the author.

Under no circumstances will any legal responsibility or blame be held against the publisher for any reparation, damages, or monetary loss due to the information herein, either directly or indirectly.

Legal Notice:
This book is copyright protected. This is only for personal use. You cannot amend, dis-tribute, sell, use, quote or paraphrase any part or the content within this book without the consent of the author.

Disclaimer Notice:
Please note the information contained within this document is for educational and entertainment purposes only. Every attempt has been made to provide accurate, up to date and reliable complete information. Readers acknowledge that the author is not engaging in the rendering of legal, financial, medical or professional advice. The content of this book has been derived from various sources. Please consult a licensed professional before attempting any techniques outlined in this book.

By reading this document, the reader agrees that under no circumstances is the author responsible for any losses, direct or indirect, which are incurred as a result of the use of information contained within this document.

Table of Contents

Introduction 4

Chapter One: Getting Started with ASP.NET Core 20

Chapter Two: Understanding Web API Basics 35

Chapter Three: Routing in ASP.NET Core 49

Chapter Four: Controllers and Actions 64

Chapter Five: Request Handling and Responses 82

Chapter Six: Middleware in ASP.NET Core 97

Chapter Seven: Managing Dependencies 112

Chapter Eight: Database Connectivity 129

Chapter Nine: Authentication and Authorization 145

Chapter Ten: Testing Web APIs 160

Chapter Eleven: API Versioning and Documentation 177

Chapter Twelve: Enhancing API Performance 191

Chapter Thirteen: Deploying ASP.NET Core Web APIs 207

Conclusion 224

Introduction

Purpose of the book

"ASP.NET Core: A Beginner's Guide to Efficient Web APIs with ASP.NET Core" emerges from a critical observation: the digital world is evolving, and with it, the need for high-performance, scalable, and efficient web applications. As a robust and versatile framework, ASP.NET Core stands out as a top contender to address these needs, boasting high performance, open-source contributions, and cross-platform capabilities. This book is crafted with the intention to arm beginners with the essential skills and knowledge to leverage these attributes, thereby laying a solid foundation for building API-driven web solutions.

Purpose of the Book

This guide aims to demystify the complexities of developing Web APIs by breaking down essential concepts into digestible and manageable lessons. It serves as both a thorough instructional manual and a foundational guide, designed to imbue readers not just with practical coding skills but also with a deep understanding of the architectural patterns and best practices that underscore robust web development.

The focus is narrowed to Web APIs to address the growing demand driven by mobile apps, IoT devices, and an increasingly interconnected array of technologies. These APIs are pivotal, enabling diverse applications to communicate and function seamlessly together. ASP.NET Core offers a streamlined, feature-rich environment for crafting these APIs, supporting lightweight HTTP services and extensive content negotiation—key components for today's web applications.

Educational Approach

The book's structure is meticulously crafted to ensure a progressive learning curve. It begins by cementing a strong understanding of ASP.NET Core's infrastructure and its core capabilities, coupled with an introduction to C# in this context. Subsequent chapters delve into more intricate subjects such as routing, middleware, data management, and security. The progression is natural—each new chapter builds upon the last, introducing increasingly complex topics while reinforcing core principles.

Integrated throughout the book are copious code examples and practical exercises designed to encourage active engagement with the material. For example:

```
public void Configure(IApplicationBuilder app, IWebHostEnvironment env)
{
    if (env.IsDevelopment())
    {
        app.UseDeveloperExceptionPage();
    }

    app.UseRouting();

    app.UseEndpoints(endpoints =>
    {
        endpoints.MapGet("/", async context =>
        {
            await context.Response.WriteAsync("Hello World!");
        });
    });
}
```

This snippet provides a glimpse into setting up middleware to handle HTTP requests, illustrating the configuration of routing and endpoints—critical components in any Web API.

Reader Engagement and Practical Application

To solidify understanding, readers are encouraged to construct their own API projects as they progress through the book. These projects not only serve as practical applications of the covered material but also reflect real-world software development practices, fostering a deeper understanding through iterative, hands-on experience.

Conclusion

Ultimately, "ASP.NET Core: A Beginner's Guide to Efficient Web APIs with ASP.NET Core" aims to do more than educate—it seeks to inspire and cultivate a new generation of developers. These readers are expected to evolve into thoughtful, innovative architects who are adept at using ASP.NET Core to develop web applications that are efficient, scalable, and secure. By the end of this book, beginners should be poised to tackle professional challenges, delve deeper into specialized subjects, and actively contribute to the developer community.

Overview of ASP.NET Core

ASP.NET Core signifies a pivotal advancement in Microsoft's suite of web development tools, aligning with the current trends towards more agile, resilient, and adaptable frameworks required by today's software architectures. This framework is open-source and cross-platform, designed specifically for constructing modern, cloud-ready, and interconnected applications such as web platforms, IoT systems, and mobile backends.

Developed to streamline and enhance the scalability of applications, ASP.NET Core supports deployments both in the cloud and on-premises, functioning seamlessly across multiple operating systems including Windows, macOS, and Linux. This ensures that applications remain independent of any specific hosting platform.

High Performance

A defining characteristic of ASP.NET Core is its exceptional performance. Benchmarking studies by TechEmpower show that ASP.NET Core consistently outperforms most other web application frameworks. This high level of performance is crafted through architectural choices focused on efficiency and the ability to handle extensive throughput while maintaining responsiveness and scalability. For instance, the following code outlines how ASP.NET Core applications can be configured for optimal performance:

```
public static IHostBuilder CreateHostBuilder(string[] args) =>
    Host.CreateDefaultBuilder(args)
        .ConfigureWebHostDefaults(webBuilder =>
        {
            webBuilder.UseStartup<Startup>();
        });
```

This snippet is indicative of the streamlined setup that enhances both performance and usability in production environments.

Dependency Injection

Dependency Injection (DI) is a core aspect of ASP.NET Core, integrating this design pattern directly into the framework. DI facilitates the external creation of dependent objects, which are then supplied to a class via constructor injection, methods, or properties. This built-in support for DI simplifies application architecture by reducing dependency on external libraries for managing these dependencies.

Middleware Pipeline

ASP.NET Core introduces a middleware pipeline where a series of request delegates process in sequence. This feature grants developers granular control over the handling of HTTP requests within their applications, through a customizable sequence of middleware components.

```csharp
public void Configure(IApplicationBuilder app)
{
    app.UseRouting();

    app.UseAuthorization();

    app.UseEndpoints(endpoints =>
    {
    endpoints.MapControllers();
    });
}
```

Above, the configuration of middleware illustrates how ASP.NET Core manages routing, authorization, and controller mapping effectively.

Cross-Platform Capabilities

As containerization and microservices become more prevalent, the need for frameworks that perform consistently across various platforms is more critical than ever. ASP.NET Core's cross-platform capabilities ensure it operates effectively whether on Windows, Linux, or macOS.

Open-Source and Community-Focused

ASP.NET Core thrives on its open-source model, with its development driven by contributions from a global community of developers on GitHub. This approach ensures that the framework is continually refined and updated in response to developer needs and industry trends.

Forward Compatibility

Microsoft's commitment to maintaining forward compatibility with ASP.NET Core ensures that future updates do not disrupt existing applications, allowing developers to rely on the framework for long-term projects.

Conclusion

ASP.NET Core is redefined from the bottom up to meet the stringent requirements of modern web applications, making it ideal for developers aiming to build efficient, scalable, and high-performance web solutions. Its commitment to being open-source and supported by a vibrant community ensures it remains at the forefront of technology advancements. This detailed exploration underscores ASP.NET Core's position as an essential framework for developers committed to delivering superior web applications.

What are Web APIs?

Web Application Programming Interfaces (Web APIs) are critical tools in contemporary software development, designed to enable smooth communication between different software systems across a network. These interfaces act as conduits, employing a set of established protocols and rules that allow web servers and clients to interact effectively, exchanging data and executing functionalities via specific endpoints.

Fundamental Role of Web APIs

At their core, Web APIs extend the capabilities of a web server by making accessible a variety of endpoints through which clients can perform actions like retrieving, updating, or processing data. This interaction typically happens over the HTTP protocol, with data being transmitted in universally recognized formats such as JSON or XML. This standardization ensures that Web APIs can serve a broad array of clients, from browsers to mobile apps and beyond, facilitating seamless interactions across different platforms.

Web APIs are pivotal in crafting enriched, responsive web applications that can dynamically fetch data without requiring full page refreshes. They also enable the construction of service-oriented architectures where services, regardless of their underlying technologies, can interact fluidly and efficiently.

How Web APIs Operate

Consider a scenario where a mobile app needs to obtain the weather forecast for a specific city. It sends an HTTP GET request to a Web API, which processes this request and returns the relevant weather data. Here's a basic coding example within the ASP.NET Core framework to depict this:

```csharp
[ApiController]
[Route("[controller]")]
public class WeatherForecastController : ControllerBase
{
    [HttpGet("{city}")]
    public ActionResult<WeatherForecast> GetWeatherByCity(string city)
    {
        WeatherForecast forecast = WeatherService.GetForecast(city);
        return Ok(forecast);
    }
}
```

In this code, a GET request to /WeatherForecast/{city} retrieves the weather data for a given city, facilitated by the WeatherService.GetForecast(city) method.

Advantages of Web APIs

The implementation of Web APIs brings several strategic benefits essential for modern digital applications:

1. **Platform Neutrality**: The reliance on standard HTTP methods enables Web APIs to interface with any client capable of making HTTP requests, enhancing their cross-platform utility.

2. **Data Efficiency**: By transmitting data in compact formats like JSON or XML, Web APIs optimize bandwidth usage, which is crucial in constrained environments.

3. **Service-Oriented Architecture Compatibility**: Web APIs are foundational in applications that adhere to SOA principles, allowing for the development of independently functioning services that can easily communicate.

4. **Scalable Architecture**: Web APIs facilitate the separation of client and server functionalities, which simplifies scaling and improves system manageability.

5. **Robust Security**: Techniques such as HTTPS encryption, token-based authentication, and OAuth ensure secure data exchanges between clients and servers.

Challenges Faced by Web APIs

Despite their extensive benefits, Web APIs can pose several challenges. These include ensuring performance and security, maintaining scalable and reliable service, and managing the complexity of different standards and protocols. Additionally, API versioning must be handled carefully to integrate new features without disrupting existing services.

Conclusive Thoughts

In essence, Web APIs are indispensable in modern web development, powering everything from simple web applications to complex enterprise solutions. They allow for the efficient and secure exchange of data and functionalities across different platforms, fostering the development of integrated, service-oriented architectures. By enabling diverse applications to communicate and share resources, Web APIs not only streamline current technological operations but also pave the way for future innovations in digital services.

How the book is organized

In the rapidly evolving field of technology, a well-crafted educational resource can make a significant difference in understanding complex software development concepts. "ASP.NET Core: A Beginner's Guide to Efficient Web APIs with ASP.NET Core" is carefully designed to navigate newcomers from basic to more advanced aspects within the ASP.NET Core framework.

Structured Learning Progression

The book is strategically laid out to enable a natural progression in learning, starting from fundamental concepts and moving towards more intricate aspects, building a robust foundation before advancing to more complex features of ASP.NET Core.

1. **Introduction to ASP.NET Core**: The opening section introduces the framework, its historical context, its benefits compared to other frameworks, and sets expectations for the journey through the book.

2. **Setting Up the Development Tools**: The first few chapters guide readers through configuring their development environment, including installations and setups crucial for beginning development. An example:

```csharp
// Example code for a basic ASP.NET Core application setup
public class Program
{
    public static void Main(string[] args)
    {
        CreateHostBuilder(args).Build().Run();
    }

    public static IHostBuilder CreateHostBuilder(string[] args) =>
        Host.CreateDefaultBuilder(args)
            .ConfigureWebHostDefaults(webBuilder =>
            {
                webBuilder.UseStartup<Startup>();
            });
}
```

This code demonstrates the initial setup of an ASP.NET Core application, providing a practical starting point that is expanded upon throughout the book.

3. **Understanding Web APIs**: Following the setup, the book covers fundamental concepts of Web APIs including HTTP basics and RESTful design tailored for ASP.NET Core.

4. **Crafting Your First Web API**: This section offers step-by-step guidance on developing a Web API, including detailed instructions on request handling, routing, and controller configuration.

5. **Advanced Data Management**: As readers advance, they explore complex data operations using Entity Framework Core, learning to perform CRUD operations and manage databases effectively.

6. **Enhancing Security**: The book progresses into sophisticated security measures for Web APIs,

discussing authentication, authorization, and the implementation of secure tokens and OAuth.

7. **Effective Testing and Documentation**: Emphasizing best practices, this part teaches readers to conduct rigorous testing and create thorough documentation for their Web APIs using tools like xUnit and Swagger.

8. **Diving into Advanced Topics**: Later sections tackle more complex subjects such as API versioning, application deployment, and performance tuning.

9. **Preparation for Future Trends**: The final chapters forecast upcoming trends in Web API development and advocate for continuous learning and adaptation in software development.

Emphasis on Practical Engagement

The narrative throughout the book strongly focuses on hands-on learning. Theoretical concepts are intertwined with practical examples, coding exercises, and real world scenarios, encouraging readers to apply their knowledge actively. Additional insights, common pitfalls, and professional practices are discussed to enrich the learning process.

Additional Educational Enhancements

To aid comprehension and retention, the book is supplemented with:

- **Illustrative Diagrams and Infographics**: These visual tools help simplify complex ideas.

- **Diverse Coding Examples**: From basic snippets to full-scale applications, these examples cater to a range of complexities.

- **Interactive Challenges**: Each chapter concludes with practical projects or challenges that prompt readers to utilize their new skills creatively.

Conclusion

"ASP.NET Core: A Beginner's Guide to Efficient Web APIs with ASP.NET Core" is methodically organized not just to impart knowledge of ASP.NET Core but to inspire confidence and innovative thinking among budding developers. By the end of the book, readers are not merely skilled in ASP.NET Core techniques but are also equipped to explore further complexities and continue their learning journey in the dynamic landscape of software development.

What you will learn

Diving into "ASP.NET Core: A Beginner's Guide to Efficient Web APIs with ASP.NET Core" equips readers with a comprehensive toolkit for mastering the intricacies of ASP.NET Core, specifically tailored to building, optimizing, and maintaining Web APIs. This guide breaks down complex technical details into digestible segments, paired with practical examples, to ensure learners develop a robust understanding and hands-on expertise adaptable to shifting tech trends.

Understanding the Basics of ASP.NET Core

The book starts with a thorough introduction to the architecture of ASP.NET Core, illustrating its improvements over the traditional .NET framework. It covers essential elements such as middleware, dependency injection, and system configuration, laying the groundwork for more advanced topics. Early on, readers engage with practical coding to understand the framework's modularity and functionality:

```csharp
public void Configure(IApplicationBuilder app)
{
    app.UseHttpsRedirection();
    app.UseRouting();
    app.UseAuthorization();
    app.UseEndpoints(endpoints =>
    {
        endpoints.MapControllers();
    });
}
```

This example demonstrates how to set up essential middleware that helps manage HTTP requests securely and efficiently, highlighting ASP.NET Core's configurability.

Crafting Effective Web APIs

The book places significant emphasis on the practical development of Web APIs. It guides readers through the essentials of creating routes, establishing controllers, and formulating methods that perform operations on data, with a focus on RESTful design to ensure the APIs are scalable and maintainable.

Mastering Data Management with Entity Framework

Managing data effectively is crucial, and the book educates readers on leveraging Entity Framework Core for robust data operations. It includes comprehensive guidance on using LINQ for database interactions, performing migrations, and executing CRUD operations, all through detailed practical exercises.

Enhancing Security

Recognizing the importance of security, the guide explores ASP.NET Core's robust authentication options, including cookie-based authentication, JWTs, and OAuth2, providing readers with the necessary knowledge to secure their APIs effectively against unauthorized access.

Focus on Testing and Documentation

The book underscores the importance of testing and proper documentation to ensure APIs are reliable and maintainable. It teaches readers how to implement unit tests using xUnit and how to document APIs using Swagger/OpenAPI, ensuring that services are well-understood and easier to use by others.

Exploring Advanced Features

As readers become more comfortable with basic concepts, the book delves into more advanced topics like API versioning, performance optimization, and deployment strategies, incorporating contemporary tools like Docker and cloud platforms such as Azure.

Preparing for Future Developments

Anticipating future trends, the concluding chapters discuss the potential of microservices and the integration of machine learning with web applications, preparing readers to navigate and lead in the evolving landscape of technology.

Conclusion

Upon completing "ASP.NET Core: A Beginner's Guide to Efficient Web APIs with ASP.NET Core," learners will not only understand how to effectively develop and manage Web APIs but will also be equipped to address complex software development challenges in real-world settings. This book provides more than just technical skills; it offers insights into problem-solving, system optimization, and designing scalable, high-quality software solutions that are prepared for future technological advancements.

Chapter One

Getting Started with ASP.NET Core

Introduction to ASP.NET Core

ASP.NET Core, unveiled by Microsoft in 2016, has rapidly become an indispensable framework for developers focused on crafting sophisticated web applications and services. Tailored to support robust, scalable, and efficient development, ASP.NET Core is now a staple in modern software engineering. This introduction delves into the framework's architecture, key features, and highlights its superiority over earlier versions and other web development frameworks.

Development and Core Philosophy

ASP.NET Core was created to meet the evolving demands of modern software projects, marking a shift towards a more agile and performance-driven framework. It's entirely open-source and supports development across multiple operating systems such as Windows, Linux, and macOS. The framework's modular approach lets developers integrate only the components they need, streamlining application construction and making management simpler.

Key Features and Upgrades

ASP.NET Core introduces several key upgrades and new functionalities to enhance development efficiency:

- **Cross-Platform Capability:** The framework enables developers to create and deploy applications on any significant platform, thereby broadening deployment options.

- **Integrated MVC and Web API Frameworks:** ASP.NET Core simplifies several development processes by merging MVC and Web API into one coherent framework, streamlining operations like routing and URL generation.

- **Enhanced Performance:** ASP.NET Core is optimized for speed, significantly outperforming many traditional frameworks with its efficient request handling.

- **Native Dependency Injection:** Incorporating dependency injection by default, the framework encourages cleaner and more maintainable code practices.

- **Adaptive Configuration System:** ASP.NET Core features a robust configuration system that adjusts smoothly across different environments such as development, staging, and production.

- **Tag Helpers:** These enhance the functionality of Razor views by making HTML element creation in server-side code easier and more intuitive.

Here's a simple example that illustrates setting up an ASP.NET Core application:

```csharp
public class Program
{
    public static void Main(string[] args)
    {
        CreateHostBuilder(args).Build().Run();
    }

    public static IHostBuilder CreateHostBuilder(string[] args) =>
        Host.CreateDefaultBuilder(args)
            .ConfigureWebHostDefaults(webBuilder =>
            {
                webBuilder.UseStartup<Startup>();
            });
}
```

This snippet shows how to configure a web host essential for handling HTTP requests in ASP.NET Core. The **Startup** class is crucial as it configures services and defines the application's request handling pipeline.

Competitive Edge

ASP.NET Core stands out for several compelling reasons:

- **Performance Efficiency:** Designed for high efficiency, it processes requests faster than many competitors, thanks to its streamlined architecture.

- **Robust Security:** Security is a central feature, with built-in mechanisms that protect against common vulnerabilities and ongoing updates to tackle new security challenges.

- **Extensive Ecosystem:** As a part of the broader .NET ecosystem, ASP.NET Core benefits from a vibrant community, extensive documentation, and a rich array of libraries and tools that bolster developer productivity and enhance application functionalities.

Conclusion

ASP.NET Core represents a significant evolution in the landscape of web development frameworks, tailored to the needs of contemporary development projects. It facilitates rapid development cycles and ensures that applications are scalable, maintainable, and secure. This positions ASP.NET Core as a preferred framework for developers and organizations committed to deploying cutting-edge web applications.

Setting up the development environment

Setting up a development environment for ASP.NET Core is crucial, as it impacts the overall productivity and success of web application development projects. This foundational step ensures developers can efficiently develop, test, and deploy applications across various platforms. Below, we explore how to configure an optimal environment tailored specifically for ASP.NET Core.

Selection of Operating System

ASP.NET Core supports a cross-platform approach, functioning effectively on Windows, Linux, and macOS. The operating system chosen often depends on the developer's personal preference or the specific requirements of their project:

- **Windows:** Known for its robust integration with ASP.NET Core, especially when paired with Visual Studio, which provides extensive .NET support and powerful project management and debugging tools.

- **Linux and macOS:** These systems are favored for their strong command-line tools and are typically chosen in environments where the deployment is targeted on Linux servers.

Software Installation Requirements

1. **.NET SDK:** The .NET SDK includes all necessary components for developing, compiling, and running ASP.NET Core applications and houses the .NET CLI, essential for project management.

The .NET SDK can be downloaded from the official .NET download page, selecting the version appropriate for the operating system in use.

2. **Integrated Development Environment (IDE):** An IDE can drastically improve the development experience by offering advanced code editing, interface design, server management, debugging, and performance analysis. Popular IDE choices for ASP.NET Core include:

- **Visual Studio:** Ideal for Windows users, offering a comprehensive suite of .NET development tools.

- **Visual Studio Code:** A versatile, open-source editor that supports C# via extensions such as C# for Visual Studio Code (powered by OmniSharp), suitable for all major platforms.

- **Rider:** A cross-platform IDE from JetBrains that equips developers with sophisticated features akin to Visual Studio.

3. Database Systems: Since many web applications require database interaction, selecting a suitable database system is essential. Developers often opt for SQL Server, PostgreSQL, or MySQL based on compatibility with their operating system and project needs.

Tool Configuration

Configuring the development tools to ensure they function together seamlessly is critical.

1. IDE Configuration: Adjust the IDE settings to recognize the .NET SDK, and ensure the IDE is set up for efficient project template use and smooth build and debug processes. For Visual Studio Code, this involves installing and configuring the C# extension to work correctly with the .NET SDK.

2. Setting Environment Variables: Proper environment variable configuration is crucial, especially for PATH settings, which enable the operating system to locate the .NET CLI and other tools from any command-line interface.

3. Database Integration: This step involves configuring the database connections by setting up connection strings within the application's configuration files and ensuring the IDE is prepared to manage database-related tasks like Entity Framework migrations.

Environment Validation

To confirm that the environment is properly configured, it is beneficial to run a simple "Hello World" ASP.NET Core project:

```
dotnet new webApp -o HelloWorld
cd HelloWorld
dotnet run
```

Executing these commands sets up and runs a new ASP.NET Core web application. Visiting **http://localhost:5000** in a web browser should display the ASP.NET Core default welcome page, indicating the environment is correctly set up.

Conclusion

Setting up the development environment correctly is fundamental for effective ASP.NET Core development, ensuring a seamless workflow from development through to deployment. This setup not only enhances developer productivity but also ensures that the applications developed are robust, reliable, and ready for deployment across various environments. A well-configured development environment is essential for developers to focus their efforts on creating high-quality web applications.

Your first ASP.NET Core application

Embarking on the creation of your first ASP.NET Core application marks a significant milestone in your journey as a developer, offering a hands-on introduction to crafting modern, scalable, and efficient web applications. This guide will walk you through the basics of setting up a simple project, providing insights into the fundamental workings and architecture of ASP.NET Core. By the end of this process, you'll have a functional web application and a solid grasp of the framework's core principles.

Necessary Preparations

Before diving into development, make sure your setup is complete. This involves having the .NET SDK installed on your system and selecting a suitable IDE such as Visual Studio, Visual Studio Code, or JetBrains Rider, each of which offers comprehensive development features that integrate well with .NET Core.

Initiating the Project

Begin by opening your terminal or command prompt, create a new directory for your project, and navigate into it. Execute the following command to generate a new ASP.NET Core web application:

```
dotnet new webapp -n MyFirstApp
```

This command utilizes the "webapp" template to create a project named "MyFirstApp." It includes a basic structure typical of ASP.NET Core applications, encompassing several essential files that you'll use throughout the development process.

Exploring the Project Files

Once your project is set up, open it in your chosen IDE and familiarize yourself with the key components:

- **Program.cs**: Houses the entry point of the application, setting up the web host which manages the processing of requests.

- **Startup.cs**: Configures services and the request handling pipeline, where middleware components are specified.

- **appsettings.json**: Stores configuration settings like connection strings, which can vary between development environments.

- **wwwroot**: Contains static assets such as HTML, CSS, JavaScript, and images, served directly to clients.

- **Pages or Controllers and Views**: Depending on the project template used, this will include Razor pages or MVC controllers and views responsible for responding to client requests.

Code Breakdown

Inspect the **Program.cs** file to understand the application's setup:

```csharp
public static void Main(string[] args)
{
    CreateHostBuilder(args).Build().Run();
}

public static IHostBuilder CreateHostBuilder(string[] args) =>
    Host.CreateDefaultBuilder(args)
        .ConfigureWebHostDefaults(webBuilder =>
        {
            webBuilder.UseStartup<Startup>();
        });
```

This snippet illustrates the construction and execution of a web host using default configurations ideal for most apps. The UseStartup<Startup>() method indicates that the **Startup** class configures services and the request pipeline.

Examine **Startup.cs** for its critical functions:

- **ConfigureServices**: Adds services to the DI container, essential for enabling loosely coupled design and easier testing.

- **Configure**: Establishes the request processing pipeline with various middleware for error handling, static file serving, and routing.

Running the Application

To launch your application, use the terminal to run the following within your project directory:

```
dotnet run
```

After compiling and initiating the application, access it by navigating to **http://localhost:5000** in your web browser to see the application live.

Enhancing Your Application

With your basic application up and running, you can begin adding more features:

- Develop additional pages or APIs.
- Connect your app to a database using Entity Framework Core.
- Add authentication and authorization to secure your app.
- Incorporate CSS frameworks like Bootstrap to style your app.

Conclusion

Building your first ASP.NET Core application provides a practical platform to learn about and experiment with the framework's capabilities. This initial project lays the groundwork for further exploration and more complex developments, allowing you to deepen your understanding of ASP.NET Core and expand your skills as a web developer.

Overview of the project structure

Understanding the structure of an ASP.NET Core project is pivotal for developers engaging with this robust framework. Familiarity with how the project components are arranged greatly aids in managing development workflows and ensures that applications are scalable and maintainable. This overview delves into the layout and key components of an ASP.NET Core project, detailing the role each plays in building effective web applications.

Key Elements of an ASP.NET Core Project

Program.cs

This foundational file is where the application begins execution. It houses the **Main** method that initializes and runs the web host, crucial for handling incoming HTTP requests. Configuration of the web host within this file sets the stage for how services and settings are handled throughout the application lifecycle.

Example:

```csharp
public class Program
{
    public static void Main(string[] args)
    {
        CreateHostBuilder(args).Build().Run();
    }

    public static IHostBuilder CreateHostBuilder(string[] args) =>
        Host.CreateDefaultBuilder(args)
            .ConfigureWebHostDefaults(webBuilder =>
            {
                webBuilder.UseStartup<Startup>();
            });
}
```

Startup.cs

Here, the application's services and middleware pipeline are configured. It features the **ConfigureServices** method to add services to the dependency injection container and the **Configure** method to define how requests are processed through various middleware components.

Example:

```csharp
public class Startup
{
    public void ConfigureServices(IServiceCollection services)
    {
        services.AddRazorPages();
    }

    public void Configure(IApplicationBuilder app, IWebHostEnvironment env)
    {
        if (env.IsDevelopment())
        {
            app.UseDeveloperExceptionPage();
        }
        else
        {
            app.UseExceptionHandler("/Error");
        }

        app.UseStaticFiles();

        app.UseRouting();

        app.UseAuthorization();

        app.UseEndpoints(endpoints =>
        {
            endpoints.MapRazorPages();
        });
    }
}
```

appsettings.json
This configuration file is crucial for storing settings that need to be different across various environments, like connection strings or application parameters. Specific settings for development, staging, and production can be differentiated using files such as **appsettings.Development.json** and **appsettings.Production.json**.

wwwroot
This directory is designated for static assets, including HTML, CSS, JavaScript, and images. Items placed here are accessible to clients and are essential for the front-end part of the application.

Controllers or Pages
The structure of the project will contain either Controllers or Pages, depending on whether it uses the MVC approach or Razor Pages:

- **Controllers**: These classes manage request handling, executing actions, and generating responses, usually returning views.

- **Pages**: In Razor Pages projects, the processing logic and user interface components are combined into single files, which simplifies page-focused application architectures.

Views or Razor Pages

In MVC-styled projects, **Views** are stored in **.cshtml** files within the Views folder, arranged by controller and including a **Shared** folder for layouts and components used across various views. For Razor Pages, this integration of view and backend logic into single files simplifies management and development within the **Pages** directory.

Models

This directory typically contains classes that define the essential business data structures of the application. This includes entities for database interaction and view models designed for transferring data between the backend operations and the front-end views.

Conclusion

The structured framework of an ASP.NET Core project is designed to support effective development of extensive, enterprise-level applications. Thoroughly understanding this structure is crucial for developers to navigate the framework effectively, ensuring that the web applications they develop are well-organized, scalable, and maintainable. Such foundational knowledge is instrumental in maximizing the benefits of ASP.NET Core for sophisticated web development projects.

Chapter Two

Understanding Web API Basics

What is a Web API?

A Web API (Application Programming Interface) is an essential framework that enables seamless interaction between different software systems across the web, crucial for creating connected web services like applications. It effectively allows external systems to access an application's functionalities and data, supporting operations such as retrieve, update, create, and delete via the internet.

Introduction to Web API

"API" stands for Application Programming Interface, a term widely recognized across the software industry to denote interfaces that simplify interactions with software components. Web APIs build upon this idea by extending these interactions over the internet through the HTTP protocol, which facilitates data transfer across diverse systems, enhancing software application capabilities.

Operational Mechanics of Web APIs

Web APIs operate by establishing endpoints that handle HTTP requests and deliver responses using methods like GET, POST, PUT, and DELETE. The data exchanged in these transactions is typically formatted in JSON or XML, making it easily readable and exchangeable.

Consider a practical example where a Web API is set up to manage a digital book library. It could provide an HTTP endpoint enabling users to retrieve a list of books via a GET request or add a new book using a POST request. Below is a conceptual example using C# within the ASP.NET Core framework, commonly used for building robust Web APIs:

```
[Route("api/[controller]")]
[ApiController]
public class BooksController : ControllerBase
{
    private readonly IBookService _bookService;

    public BooksController(IBookService bookService)
    {
        _bookService = bookService;
    }

    [HttpGet]
    public ActionResult<List<Book>> GetAllBooks()
    {
        return _bookService.GetAllBooks();
    }

    [HttpPost]
    public ActionResult<Book> AddBook([FromBody] Book newBook)
    {
        var book = _bookService.AddBook(newBook);
        return CreatedAtAction(nameof(GetBook), new { id = book.Id }, book);
    }
}
```

This snippet from the **BooksController** demonstrates how various HTTP requests are processed, with each method mapped to specific functionalities like retrieving all books or adding a new one.

Advantages of Web APIs

Interoperability: Web APIs facilitate the interaction between different applications regardless of their underlying technologies, enabling seamless system integration.

Accessibility: Utilizing standard HTTP protocols, Web APIs can be accessed by a diverse range of clients, including web browsers and mobile apps.

Scalability: Designed to handle numerous requests simultaneously, Web APIs are perfectly suited for large-scale services that operate over the internet.

Efficiency: By enabling direct data and functionality sharing between applications, Web APIs reduce redundancy and enhance the speed of system interactions.

Use Cases for Web APIs

Web APIs are utilized across a broad range of industries and applications:

- **Mobile apps** that require server-side data retrieval.
- **E-commerce platforms** that perform transactions by interacting with external applications.
- **IoT systems** that depend on server-side applications for data processing and monitoring.

Conclusion

Web APIs are fundamental to contemporary software architecture, allowing diverse applications to communicate and interact over the internet. Their role in facilitating connected, efficient, and scalable interactions is indispensable in today's interconnected digital environment. By providing the means to integrate various systems dynamically, Web APIs empower developers to construct sophisticated, comprehensive solutions that span across multiple platforms and applications.

Principles of REST

REST (Representational State Transfer) is a design approach that harnesses the capabilities of HTTP methodologies to build web services. It is characterized not by the technologies it employs, but by an architectural style that defines several constraints. These principles guide the design of web architectures that are scalable, simple, and lightweight, making RESTful services highly favored for public API development.

Fundamental Principles of REST

Client-Server Separation: A key characteristic of REST is the separation of concerns between the client and the server. This separation allows the client to handle the user interface independently, while the server manages the backend processes. This division not only enhances flexibility but also allows for scalability since both components can develop independently of one another.

Statelessness: REST requires that each request from the client to the server contains all the information necessary to execute the request, without the server needing to remember previous requests. This statelessness facilitates greater reliability and scalability as the server does not need to manage session states, making it easier to manage and scale the server independently.

Cacheability: Caching is a significant aspect of RESTful architectures, enabling high performance and scalability. Responses must therefore define themselves as cacheable or non-cacheable, making a well-managed cache a crucial element in network efficiency. Caching can eliminate the need for some client-server interactions, reducing the number of requests to the server.

Uniform Interface: The principle of a uniform interface simplifies the architecture by decoupling the implementation and the services it offers. This uniformity requires that:

1. **Resources are uniquely identified through their URIs** in requests.

2. **Representations manipulate resources**: When a client has a representation, it has enough details to modify or delete the resource on the server.

3. **Messages are self-descriptive**: Information about how to process a message is contained within it, using standard methods like HTTP.

4. **HATEOAS (Hypermedia as the Engine of Application State)**: Clients interact with a RESTful service dynamically through hypermedia provided dynamically by application servers.

Layered System: REST allows for a layered architecture where interactions can occur through multiple intermediary servers. This layering increases security and scalability, as servers can balance loads and encrypt data.

Code on Demand (optional): An optional constraint of REST, allowing servers to extend client functionality by sending code to the client to be executed. This may include compiled components or scripts enhancing the client capabilities temporarily.

Example of a RESTful Exchange

Consider a simple RESTful exchange where a client makes an HTTP GET request to retrieve a user's details:

```
GET /users/1234 HTTP/1.1
Host: api.example.com
Accept: application/json
```

The server responds with the resource details:

```
HTTP/1.1 200 OK
Content-Type: application/json
Content-Length: 140
```

```
{
  "userId": "1234",
  "username": "johndoe",
  "email": "john.doe@example.com"
}
```

In this scenario, the client requests specific user information using a unique identifier, and the server responds with the user data in JSON format.

Conclusion

The REST architectural style plays a pivotal role in developing web services that are simple, maintainable, and scalable. By adhering to REST principles, developers can create web services that are not only powerful and flexible but also integrate smoothly with other web technologies. This alignment with the foundational principles of the web itself allows for robust and extensible architectures, ensuring that applications can grow and evolve over time.

HTTP fundamentals

Hypertext Transfer Protocol (HTTP) is the foundational protocol that facilitates data exchange on the World Wide Web, supporting the transfer of multimedia content like HTML files, images, and videos. Originating in 1991, HTTP has undergone several revisions, with HTTP/2 as the most recent standardized version and HTTP/3 being actively developed. For those in web development and networking fields, a deep grasp of HTTP is crucial as it drives the fundamental mechanisms of web communication.

Basic Principles of HTTP

HTTP is based on a client-server model, where a client such as a web browser sends a request to a server which hosts a web application. The server processes this request and sends back a response. This protocol specifies how messages should be formatted and transmitted, and defines the actions that web servers and browsers are expected to perform.

HTTP Communication Components

HTTP Requests: These are initiated by the client to interact with resources on a server, identified by URLs. Components of a request include:

- **Method:** Indicates the requested action (GET, POST, PUT, DELETE, HEAD) to be performed on the resource.

- **URL/URI:** Specifies the location of the resource on the server.

- **HTTP Version:** Indicates the protocol version, such as HTTP/1.1 or HTTP/2.

- **Headers:** Additional information about the request or the client.

- **Body (optional):** Contains data being sent to the server, usually with POST or PUT requests.

HTTP Responses: In response to a client's request, the server sends back:

- **Status Code:** Communicates the outcome of the request.

- **HTTP Version:** The version of the protocol used in the response.

- **Headers:** Metadata about the server or the response.

- **Body (optional):** Contains the requested data or content.

Overview of HTTP Methods

HTTP defines methods that specify actions to be performed on resources:

- **GET:** Requests data from the server without altering any resources.

- **HEAD:** Similar to GET, but only requests metadata and does not return a body.

- **POST:** Sends data to the server, possibly changing or creating resources.

- **PUT:** Replaces a resource entirely with the specified data.

- **DELETE:** Removes a specified resource.

- **OPTIONS:** Retrieves the communication methods supported by the server.

Classification of HTTP Status Codes

HTTP status codes are categorized to indicate the result of a request:

- **1xx (Informational):** Indicates that the request has begun processing.

- **2xx (Successful):** Confirms that the request was successfully received and processed.

- **3xx (Redirection):** Indicates additional actions are required to complete the request.

- **4xx (Client Error):** Suggests an error in the request.

- **5xx (Server Error):** Indicates a server-side error in processing the request.

HTTP Transaction Example

Here's a basic example of an HTTP GET request and the server's response:

Request:

```
GET /index.html HTTP/1.1
Host: www.example.com
```

Response:

```
HTTP/1.1 200 OK
Content-Type: text/html
Content-Length: 1354

<html>
<head>
  <title>An Example Page</title>
</head>
<body>
  Hello World, this is a very simple HTML document.
</body>
</html>
```

In this scenario, the client requests the resource "/index.html" from "www.example.com," and the server responds with the HTML content of that resource.

Conclusion

Understanding HTTP is essential for professionals in web technologies and networking, as it underpins web interactions and data transfer processes. As technology evolves, HTTP continues to develop, ensuring it meets modern demands for security and operational efficiency in digital communications.

ASP.NET Core's alignment with REST

ASP.NET Core is a powerful, open-source framework designed for building high-performance, cloud-based, internet-connected applications such as web apps, IoT apps, and mobile backends. It naturally supports the Representational State Transfer (REST) architectural style, which is prevalent in designing scalable web services.

Alignment of ASP.NET Core with REST Principles

REST, an architectural style that leverages existing web protocols and standards, primarily HTTP, emphasizes scalability, simplicity, and interaction. ASP.NET Core integrates seamlessly with these RESTful principles, enhancing its capabilities for web service development.

Client-Server Separation: ASP.NET Core facilitates a clear separation between client and server operations. The framework handles server-side processing, including HTTP request handling and response generation, while the client can be any device or front-end capable of HTTP communication. This separation allows for the independent evolution of both client-side and server-side components, boosting scalability and maintainability.

Statelessness: ASP.NET Core encourages the development of stateless applications where each HTTP request contains all necessary information independently of others. This statelessness simplifies the server architecture and enhances reliability and scalability, as the server does not maintain any client state between requests.

Cacheability: ASP.NET Core enables responses to be marked as cacheable, utilizing standard HTTP cache-control headers. This allows clients and intermediaries to cache responses appropriately, reducing the need for repeated requests and improving the efficiency and scalability of applications.

Uniform Interface: ASP.NET Core promotes a uniform interface for interacting with web resources, using standard HTTP methods such as GET, POST, PUT, and DELETE. This uniformity simplifies the interactions between clients and servers and decouples the architecture, allowing the independent evolution of components.

Layered System: Applications built with ASP.NET Core can operate within layered architectures, where clients may not directly communicate with the actual data-serving application server. This can include intermediate layers such as security controls (authentication gateways) and load balancers, which enhance security and scalability.

Code on Demand (optional): While not a commonly used REST constraint, ASP.NET Core supports sending executable code to the client, potentially extending client functionality dynamically as needed.

Example of RESTful API in ASP.NET Core

To demonstrate how ASP.NET Core adheres to REST principles, consider a simple API for managing a collection of books:

First, define a **Book** model:

```
public class Book
{
    public int Id { get; set; }
    public string Title { get; set; }
    public string Author { get; set; }
}
```

Then, develop a controller that handles standard CRUD operations:

```csharp
[Route("api/[controller]")]
[ApiController]
public class BooksController : ControllerBase
{
    private static List<Book> books = new List<Book>()
    {
        new Book { Id = 1, Title = "Learn ASP.NET Core", Author = "Microsoft" }
    };

    [HttpGet]
    public ActionResult<IEnumerable<Book>> GetAllBooks()
    {
        return books;
    }

    [HttpGet("{id}")]
    public ActionResult<Book> GetBook(int id)
    {
        var book = books.FirstOrDefault(b => b.Id == id);
        if (book == null)
        {
            return NotFound();
        }
        return book;
    }

    [HttpPost]
    public IActionResult AddBook(Book book)
    {
        books.Add(book);
        return CreatedAtAction(nameof(GetBook), new { id = book.Id }, book);
    }

    [HttpDelete("{id}")]
    public IActionResult DeleteBook(int id)
    {
```

```
    var book = books.FirstOrDefault(b => b.Id == id);
    if (book == null)
    {
        return NotFound();
    }
    books.Remove(book);
    return NoContent();
}
```

This controller showcases RESTful principles:

- Each HTTP method (GET, POST, DELETE) corresponds to standard CRUD operations.

- It uses standard HTTP status codes to communicate outcomes of API calls.

- The API is stateless, with each request being self-contained.

- Responses are clearly defined and appropriate for caching where feasible.

Conclusion

ASP.NET Core's compatibility with REST principles makes it an excellent choice for developing efficient, scalable, and maintainable web APIs. Its framework and tooling naturally support REST's best practices, empowering developers to create robust web applications and services.

Chapter Three

Routing in ASP.NET Core

Understanding routing

Routing plays a crucial role in web development, determining how a web application responds to client requests to access specific endpoints, often delineated by URLs. By directing incoming requests to the correct server-side handlers based on predefined URL patterns, routing ensures that applications are efficient, scalable, and manageable.

Overview of Routing

The process of routing involves mapping incoming requests to the correct handlers within the application, based on predefined URL patterns. This setup is essential for the effective operation of any web application, ensuring that requests are processed accurately and efficiently.

Different Routing Approaches

Routing in web applications typically falls into two main categories:

1. **Conventional Routing:** This approach utilizes predefined URL patterns to guide requests to various application components. It's particularly common in traditional web frameworks like ASP.NET MVC and is generally configured at the application's startup.

2. **Attribute Routing:** Offering a more granular control by defining routes directly on controllers or actions via attributes, this method is ideal for creating RESTful APIs where precise control over URL routes is necessary.

Implementing Routing in ASP.NET Core

ASP.NET Core supports both conventional and attribute routing, providing a comprehensive and flexible routing system suitable for a variety of web applications.

Conventional Routing

Conventional routing in ASP.NET Core is configured in the Startup.cs file, where developers can establish patterns for the application to follow when matching incoming requests.

Example of conventional routing setup in ASP.NET Core:

```
app.UseEndpoints(endpoints =>
{
    endpoints.MapControllerRoute(
        name: "default",
        pattern: "{controller=Home}/{action=Index}/{id?}");
});
```

This configuration specifies a default route where the application directs requests to a specified controller and action, with an optional id parameter.

Attribute Routing

Attribute routing enhances control by allowing routes to be defined directly on controllers or actions using attributes, making it extremely useful for APIs.

Example of attribute routing on an ASP.NET Core controller:

```csharp
[Route("api/[controller]")]
public class BooksController : ControllerBase
{
    [HttpGet]
    public IActionResult GetAllBooks()
    {
        // Method implementation
    }

    [HttpGet("{id}")]
    public IActionResult GetBookById(int id)
    {
        // Method implementation
    }

    [HttpPost]
    public IActionResult AddBook([FromBody]Book book)
    {
        // Method implementation
    }
}
```

In this controller, the [Route] attribute specifies that its actions are available under api/books, with additional attributes indicating the HTTP methods each action supports.

Benefits of Proper Routing

Well-implemented routing offers multiple advantages:

- **Maintainability:** Clear and logical routing enhances the maintainability of the application.
- **SEO and User Experience:** Well-crafted URLs improve SEO and make the application more user-friendly.

- **Performance:** Efficient routing reduces the time needed to resolve requests, boosting overall performance.

Conclusion

Effective routing is essential in defining how web applications handle and process requests. ASP.NET Core's versatile routing capabilities allow developers to implement both conventional and attribute-based routing, adapting to the needs of diverse web applications. Proper routing ensures that applications not only perform well but also remain easy to manage and scale as they evolve.

Convention-based vs. attribute routing

In web development, particularly in frameworks like ASP.NET Core, the way HTTP requests are matched to the code that handles them is governed by routing strategies. Two predominant approaches to routing are used: convention-based routing and attribute routing. Each technique offers unique benefits and fits different project requirements and developer preferences.

Convention-based Routing

Convention-based routing relies on predefined routing conventions to determine how URLs correspond to actions within the application. This method has been a staple in earlier versions of ASP.NET and is prevalent in ASP.NET Core for projects that benefit from a centralized routing configuration.

How it operates: This routing style requires routes to be defined in the application's startup configuration, using route templates that include parameters to be matched in the URL.

Example: Here's an example of setting up convention-based routing in the Startup.cs file of an ASP.NET Core application:

```csharp
public void Configure(IApplicationBuilder app, IWebHostEnvironment env)
{
    app.UseRouting();

    app.UseEndpoints(endpoints =>
    {
        endpoints.MapControllerRoute(
            name: "default",
            pattern: "{controller=Home}/{action=Index}/{id?}");
    });
}
```

This configuration sets a default route template, directing requests to specific controllers and actions, with 'Home' and 'Index' as defaults for controller and action, respectively. The 'id' parameter is optional.

Attribute Routing

Attribute routing provides a finer level of control by defining routes directly on controllers or their actions through attributes. This method is especially favored for its precision and flexibility in ASP.NET MVC 5 and subsequent versions including ASP.NET Core.

How it operates: Routes are applied directly above controllers or action methods using attributes, allowing for detailed and varied route definitions.

Example: Below is how attribute routing might look within an ASP.NET Core controller:

```csharp
[Route("api/[controller]")]
public class BooksController : ControllerBase
{
    [HttpGet]
    public IActionResult GetAllBooks()
    {
        // Method implementation
    }

    [HttpGet("{id}")]
    public IActionResult GetBookById(int id)
    {
        // Method implementation
    }

    [HttpPost]
    public IActionResult AddBook([FromBody] Book book)
    {
        // Method implementation
    }

    [HttpDelete("{id}")]
    public IActionResult DeleteBook(int id)
    {
        // Method implementation
    }
}
```

In this controller, each action is tagged with HTTP method attributes, and routes are specifically tailored, such as [HttpGet("{id}")] for fetching a book by ID.

Evaluating Convention-based vs. Attribute Routing

Flexibility:

- **Convention-based:** Less flexible as it adheres to global patterns.

- **Attribute Routing:** Highly flexible with the ability to define intricate and specific routes.

Maintainability:

- **Convention-based:** More straightforward, benefiting large projects with uniform routing patterns.
- **Attribute Routing:** Requires careful management due to potential complexity from numerous detailed routes.

Control:

- **Convention-based:** Offers less control over the individual routes.
- **Attribute Routing:** Delivers detailed control over each route configuration, suitable for complex scenarios.

Ideal Use Cases:

- **Convention-based:** Best for applications with straightforward, uniform routing needs.
- **Attribute Routing:** Ideal for complex applications, particularly APIs that demand customized route patterns.

Conclusion

The choice between convention-based and attribute routing in ASP.NET Core usually hinges on the application's specific needs and the developers' strategic preferences. Convention-based routing is simpler and well-suited for less complex applications or when a unified routing approach is advantageous. Attribute routing, offering more control and customization, is preferable for more complex applications or when precise route management is critical. Understanding the nuances of each routing type is essential for architects and developers to build effective, maintainable, and scalable web applications.

Routing constraints

Routing constraints serve as critical tools in web development, defining rules that URLs must satisfy to be routed to specific handlers. These rules ensure that incoming requests are directed to appropriate resources based on specified URL conditions, enhancing the security and functionality of applications. Such constraints are particularly valuable in frameworks like ASP.NET Core, where they help build secure and efficient web applications.

Functionality of Routing Constraints

Routing constraints limit the kinds of requests that can match a defined route pattern. Without these constraints, any request that matches a URL pattern structurally would be routed accordingly, potentially leading to unwanted or unauthorized access. By implementing routing constraints, developers ensure that URL parameters adhere to specified types, ranges, or other custom criteria essential for the application's logic.

Types of Routing Constraints

ASP.NET Core provides several built-in routing constraints that serve various validation purposes:

1. **Regex Constraint:** Checks parameters against specific regular expressions.

2. **Length Constraint:** Ensures a parameter's length falls within a specified range.

3. **Range Constraint:** Verifies that a parameter's value lies within a defined numerical range.

4. **Min/Max Constraint:** Sets minimum or maximum limits for numeric parameters.

5. **Type-Specific Constraints (Int, Float, Double, Decimal):** Ensures parameters match specific numeric types.

6. **GUID Constraint:** Confirms parameters are valid GUIDs.

7. **Bool Constraint:** Checks for boolean values in parameters.

8. **DateTime Constraint:** Ensures parameters represent valid dates.

Application of Routing Constraints in ASP.NET Core

Routing constraints in ASP.NET Core can be applied through conventional routing or attribute routing:

Conventional Routing with Constraints

For conventional routing, constraints are defined within the route setup in the **Startup.cs** file, alongside other route definitions:

```csharp
public void Configure(IApplicationBuilder app, IWebHostEnvironment env)
{
    app.UseRouting();

    app.UseEndpoints(endpoints =>
    {
        endpoints.MapControllerRoute(
            name: "default",
            pattern: "{controller}/{action}/{id?}",
            defaults: new { controller = "Home", action = "Index" },
            constraints: new { id = @"\d+" });
    });
}
```

This setup ensures that the **id** parameter accepts only digits, as specified by the **d+** regular expression. Requests with non-digit **id** values will not trigger this route.

Attribute Routing with Constraints

Attribute routing allows for directly placing constraints on controllers or actions through annotations, providing detailed control over routes:

```csharp
[Route("api/books/{id:int:min(1)}")]
public IActionResult GetBook(int id)
{
    // Method implementation
}
```

Here, the **id** parameter is constrained to integer values with a minimum of 1, ensuring that only URLs meeting these criteria are routed to this action.

Advantages of Implementing Routing Constraints

Utilizing routing constraints offers multiple benefits:

- **Enhanced Security:** They prevent processing requests with invalid or unsuitable parameters, thus reinforcing the application's security.

- **Boosted Performance:** By eliminating the processing of irrelevant or incorrect requests early, constraints improve the overall efficiency of the application.

- **Greater Reliability:** Constraints ensure that only valid and expected data is processed, aiding in the stability and reliability of the application.

Conclusion

Routing constraints are essential for effectively managing how web applications handle incoming requests, particularly ensuring that requests are valid and appropriate for the intended handlers. In environments like ASP.NET Core, routing constraints not only secure the application but also optimize its performance and reliability. These constraints enable developers to exert precise control over request handling, ensuring that the application behaves as expected in various scenarios.

Handling route conflicts

Managing route conflicts is crucial in web development to ensure that applications respond correctly to user requests.

Conflicts in routing occur when multiple routing rules could potentially match a single URL, causing ambiguity in request handling. Resolving these conflicts is essential for maintaining the application's functionality and enhancing user experience.

Recognizing Route Conflicts

Route conflicts generally emerge from:

1. **Overlapping Routes:** Occurs when multiple routes could match a URL due to similar or poorly defined patterns, often in large applications or those developed modularly.

2. **Similar Route Patterns:** Happens when routes are structurally similar but are intended for different types of data or requests, leading to confusion over the appropriate route for a URL.

Strategies for Resolving Route Conflicts

Developers can adopt several approaches to mitigate and resolve route conflicts effectively:

1. Define Routes Clearly

Developing clear, distinct route patterns is fundamental. This involves:

- **Specificity in Route Definition:** Crafting routes that are unique and explicitly define different application sections.

- **Strategic Route Ordering:** Routes are processed in the order they are defined; thus, placing specific routes before more generic ones can prevent mismatches.

2. Implement Attribute Routing

Attribute routing allows for precise route definitions on controllers and actions, offering direct control over routing paths and reducing the likelihood of conflicts.

Example:

```csharp
[Route("api/products/specials")]
public IActionResult GetSpecialProducts()
{
    // Implementation
}
```

```csharp
[Route("api/products/{id:int}")]
public IActionResult GetProductById(int id)
{
    // Implementation
}
```

In this setup, attribute routing distinctly differentiates between routes for special products and product retrieval by ID.

3. Apply Constraints to Routes

Routing constraints can differentiate routes that might otherwise overlap by specifying rules about the parameters, such as type or value range.

Example:

```csharp
[Route("api/products/{id:int}")]
public IActionResult GetProductById(int id)
{
    // Implementation
}

[Route("api/products/{category}")]
public IActionResult GetProductsByCategory(string category)
{
    // Implementation
}
```

Here, constraints ensure that numerical IDs direct requests to **GetProductById**, while string-type categories route to **GetProductsByCategory**.

4. Develop Custom Route Handlers

For complex routing needs where predefined methods fall short, custom route handlers can be developed. These handlers can contain advanced logic to dynamically determine the appropriate routing based on specific criteria.

5. Monitor and Log Routing Decisions

Setting up logging and monitoring for how routes are resolved can help detect and address unexpected behaviors or conflicts, providing insights into actual routing performance.

Best Practices

Effective route conflict management also involves several best practices:

- **Regularly Review and Refactor Routing:** As applications evolve, so should their routing to ensure clarity and minimize conflicts.

- **Centralize Routing Management:** Especially in team settings, to prevent redundant or overlapping route definitions.

- **Automate Route Testing:** Automated tests can identify potential routing issues early, helping to prevent conflicts before deployment.

Conclusion

Effectively managing route conflicts involves strategic planning and implementation of clear routing rules to ensure predictable and efficient application behavior. Utilizing clear definitions, attribute routing with constraints, custom handlers, and thorough testing and monitoring are vital to resolving potential conflicts. Regular reviews of routing strategies help maintain an application's routing integrity, crucial for seamless functionality and user satisfaction.

Chapter Four

Controllers and Actions

Role of controllers in ASP.NET Core

In ASP.NET Core, controllers are crucial for facilitating the interaction between client requests and server-side responses, operating as a core component of the Model-View-Controller (MVC) architecture. These components serve as the conduit through which the user interface and application logic interact, orchestrating the flow of data and user commands in web applications.

Overview of Controllers in ASP.NET Core

Controllers are classes designated to handle incoming HTTP requests. They are a central element in the MVC framework, where they manage the coordination between the model (data operations) and the view (UI). For API-driven applications within ASP.NET Core, controllers handle data transactions and communication without engaging with a user interface, focusing instead on data payloads.

Key Functions of Controllers

1. **Request Processing:** Controllers act as the entry point for HTTP requests, determining how these should be handled and which operations to invoke.

2. **Data Interaction:** Typically, controllers interact with data models, either directly or more commonly, via

service classes that encapsulate business logic and data access.

3. **Response Generation:** After processing the incoming requests and any necessary data manipulation, controllers generate the appropriate responses to be sent back to the client, whether as rendered views or data formats like JSON.

Structuring Controllers

Controllers are usually organized in the **Controllers** directory in an ASP.NET Core project and extend from either **Controller** or **ControllerBase**.

- **Controller:** Suitable for applications that involve rendering views. It includes support for rendering views and is primarily used in MVC applications.

- **ControllerBase:** Ideal for API services that return data (e.g., JSON, XML) and do not require view support.

Example of a MVC Controller

```
public class HomeController : Controller
{
    public IActionResult Index()
    {
        return View();
    }

    public IActionResult About()
    {
        return View();
    }
}
```

This **HomeController** demonstrates basic controller actions, returning views for the **Index** and **About** routes.

Role in API Development

In the context of API development, controllers are pivotal in managing data responses suitable for client-side applications and services, focusing on data formats rather than user interfaces.

```csharp
[Route("api/[controller]")]
[ApiController]
public class ProductsController : ControllerBase
{
    private readonly IProductService _productService;

    public ProductsController(IProductService productService)
    {
        _productService = productService;
    }

    [HttpGet]
    public ActionResult<List<Product>> GetAll()
    {
        return _productService.GetAll();
    }
}
```

```csharp
[HttpGet("{id}")]
public ActionResult<Product> Get(int id)
{
    var product = _productService.GetProductById(id);
    if (product == null)
    {
        return NotFound();
    }
    return product;
}

[HttpPost]
public IActionResult Create(Product product)
{
    _productService.AddProduct(product);
    return CreatedAtAction(nameof(Get), new { id = product.Id }, product);
}
```

In this **ProductsController**, attribute routing enhances the clarity and specificity of HTTP method handling, directly linking actions to HTTP verbs.

Best Practices

- **Streamline Controllers:** Keeping controllers focused and concise by offloading business logic and data handling to services.

- **Utilize Dependency Injection:** Leverage ASP.NET Core's dependency injection features to supply controllers with necessary services, promoting cleaner and more scalable code.

- **Single Responsibility:** Controllers should address a specific area of application functionality, simplifying maintenance and scalability.

Conclusion

Controllers are fundamental in ASP.NET Core, enabling efficient management of request handling, data processing, and response delivery, whether for web pages in MVC frameworks or data endpoints in APIs. By following best practices such as minimizing controller responsibilities and using dependency injection, developers can ensure their applications remain organized, maintainable, and effective.

Writing action methods

In ASP.NET Core, action methods are pivotal elements within controllers, tasked with responding to HTTP requests and dispatching the correct responses. These methods are integral components of the Model-View-Controller (MVC) architecture, managing the interplay between user inputs and the application's business logic. This guide outlines essential practices for crafting effective action methods, enhanced by concrete examples to demonstrate their practical implementation.

Fundamentals of Action Methods

Action methods are public functions in a controller designed to handle specific types of HTTP requests. Each method should execute a defined task, such as data retrieval, modification, or returning a response type like a view or JSON data.

Key Attributes of Action Methods

Effective action methods are marked by:

- **Purpose clarity:** Each method should have a specific, singular focus.

- **Brevity:** Methods should remain succinct, offloading complex operations to services or other application layers.

- **Intuitive naming:** Method names should clearly reflect their function, aiding code readability and maintenance.

Crafting Action Methods in ASP.NET Core

Action methods in ASP.NET Core are structured to handle various HTTP requests and return an **IActionResult** or **ActionResult<T>** for typed results, encapsulating various HTTP responses.

Standard Implementation

An action method typically processes an HTTP request and delivers a response based on that request.

Example:

```
public class ProductsController : Controller
{
    [HttpGet]
    public IActionResult Index()
```

```csharp
{
    return View();
}

[HttpGet("{id}")]
public IActionResult Details(int id)
{
    var product = productService.GetProductById(id);
    if (product == null)
    {
        return NotFound();
    }
    return View(product);
}
```

```csharp
[HttpPost]
public IActionResult Create(Product product)
{
    if (ModelState.IsValid)
    {
        productService.AddProduct(product);
        return RedirectToAction(nameof(Index));
    }
    return View(product);
}
}
```

This controller demonstrates handling of various HTTP requests, showcasing actions that render views, handle form submissions, and manage redirection.

Response Type Management

Action methods can return different types of responses to suit the application's needs:

- **ViewResult** or **PartialViewResult:** Renders full or partial views respectively.
- **JsonResult:** Outputs JSON data.

- **StatusCodeResult:** Returns HTTP status codes.
- **RedirectResult:** Redirects to a URL or another action method.

Example:

```csharp
[HttpGet("search")]
public IActionResult Search(string query)
{
    var results = productService.SearchProducts(query);
    return Json(results);
}
```

This action method exemplifies how to handle a search query and return results in JSON, useful for APIs or client-side applications utilizing AJAX.

Enhancing Methods with Model Binding

Model binding facilitates the process by automatically assigning values from HTTP requests to action method parameters.

Example:

```csharp
[HttpPost]
public IActionResult Update([FromBody] Product product)
{
    if (!ModelState.IsValid)
    {
        return BadRequest(ModelState);
    }
    productService.UpdateProduct(product);
    return NoContent();
}
```

This example uses the **[FromBody]** attribute to bind JSON data to the **Product** parameter, simplifying the method.

Best Practices for Action Methods

- **Maintain concise methods:** Action methods should focus on routing tasks, relying on services for extensive logic.

- **Use explicit routing:** Employ attribute routing to define routes directly on actions, enhancing transparency and maintainability.

- **Validate inputs rigorously:** Always validate incoming data, particularly for actions that alter data or access sensitive information.

- **Implement dependency injection effectively:** Utilize ASP.NET Core's built-in dependency injection to manage dependencies cleanly, enhancing the scalability and testability of the application.

Conclusion

Action methods are foundational to the functionality of ASP.NET Core applications, ensuring proper handling of HTTP requests and the generation of appropriate responses. By adhering to best practices—keeping action methods focused, employing clear routing and validation strategies, and effectively managing dependencies—developers can ensure their applications are robust, maintainable, and efficient.

Understanding action result

In ASP.NET Core, the concept of action results is fundamental for developers to manage and tailor the HTTP responses sent to clients. These results are pivotal for defining the content and format of the response based on the incoming request's specifics. This detailed exploration covers the various action result types within ASP.NET Core and demonstrates their application for developing adaptable and responsive web applications.

Defining Action Results

An action result in ASP.NET Core is an implementation of the **IActionResult** interface, which encapsulates the construction of an HTTP response. These are returned by controller actions to specify exactly how the server should respond to requests, including what data to return and which HTTP status codes to use.

Overview of Action Result Types

ASP.NET Core offers a range of predefined action result types to cater to various response needs:

1. **ViewResult**: Renders a view to the user, typically returning an HTML page via Razor views.

2. **PartialViewResult**: Returns a partial view, useful for updating sections of a web page dynamically through AJAX.

3. **ContentResult**: Directly returns a string with a content-type of **text/plain**, unless otherwise specified.

4. **JsonResult**: Outputs a serialized object in JSON format, commonly used in API responses.

5. **FileResult**: Facilitates file transfers to the client, handling file streams, byte arrays, or physical files.

6. **StatusCodeResult**: Allows sending specific HTTP status codes, ideal for indicating various HTTP responses explicitly.

7. **RedirectResult**: Manages client redirections to different URLs, crucial after operations like form submissions.

8. **NotFoundResult**: Delivers a 404 Not Found status, particularly when a requested resource is unavailable.

9. **OkResult**: Indicates a successful operation with a 200 OK status, used when no additional data needs to be returned.

Practical Examples

The following examples illustrate how these results might be utilized within a controller:

```
public class HomeController : Controller
{
    public IActionResult Index()
    {
        return View();  // Returns a ViewResult
    }

    public IActionResult GetJson()
    {
        var data = new { Name = "John", Age = 30 };
        return Json(data);  // Returns a JsonResult
    }

    public IActionResult DownloadFile()
    {
        var path = "path/to/file.pdf";
        return PhysicalFile(path, "application/pdf");  // Returns a FileResult
    }
```

```
public IActionResult CheckStatus(int id)
{
    if (!IsValid(id))
        return NotFound();  // Returns a NotFoundResult

    return Ok();  // Returns an OkResult
}
```

Effective Use of Action Results

- **Choose the Right Type**: It's vital to select an action result type that aligns with the specific needs of the response. For instance, choose **JsonResult** for API outputs and **ViewResult** for rendering views.

- **Utilize ControllerBase Helpers**: ASP.NET Core's ControllerBase class offers helper methods such as **Ok()**, **NotFound()**, and **File()** which simplify the instantiation of action results, making code more readable and concise.

- **Employ Status Codes in APIs**: For APIs, often a status indication (e.g., success or error) is sufficient without a data payload. Utilize **OkResult**, **NotFoundResult**, or other similar results to streamline these responses.

- **Manage Errors Effectively**: Ensure that error responses are informative and helpful, using status codes and messages to guide the user or client software.

Conclusion

Mastering action results in ASP.NET Core empowers developers to control the responses of web applications dynamically and precisely. By deploying the appropriate action results, developers can ensure that their applications respond appropriately to user interactions, whether that involves displaying content, downloading files, redirecting users, or simply communicating the outcome of a request. This capability is essential for crafting efficient, user-centric web applications that respond intelligently to a wide array of client requests.

Controller best practices

In developing web applications with ASP.NET Core, controllers act as a crucial conduit between incoming requests and the system's responses. Employing best practices in the design and implementation of controllers enhances the readability, maintainability, and performance of the code. This article provides essential guidelines for optimizing controller architecture in ASP.NET Core, illustrated with relevant code examples.

1. Maintain Slim Controllers

It's imperative to keep controllers focused on routing responsibilities and to delegate business logic and data management to services or other layers. This adherence to the Single Responsibility Principle (SRP) ensures controllers manage only HTTP request handling, improving clarity and maintainability.

Example:

```csharp
public class ProductsController : ControllerBase
{
    private readonly IProductService _productService;

    public ProductsController(IProductService productService)
    {
        _productService = productService;
    }

    [HttpGet("{id}")]
    public async Task<IActionResult> GetProduct(int id)
    {
        var product = await _productService.GetProductByIdAsync(id);
        if (product == null)
            return NotFound();

        return Ok(product);
    }
}
```

Here, the controller relies on a service to retrieve product details, keeping the action method concise and focused solely on handling the response.

2. Implement Dependency Injection

ASP.NET Core facilitates dependency injection natively, which should be utilized to introduce dependencies into controllers. This approach promotes testability and reduces coupling.

Example:

```csharp
public class OrderController : ControllerBase
{
    private readonly IOrderRepository _orderRepository;

    public OrderController(IOrderRepository orderRepository)
    {
        _orderRepository = orderRepository;
    }

    // Action methods here
}
```

This controller receives its dependencies through the constructor, enhancing modularity and simplifying unit testing.

3. Use Attribute Routing

Employing attribute routing to define explicit routes enhances the transparency and manageability of request handling, helping prevent routing conflicts.

Example:

```csharp
[Route("api/[controller]")]
public class UsersController : ControllerBase
{
    [HttpGet("profile/{userId}")]
    public IActionResult GetUserProfile(int userId)
    {
        // Implementation
    }
}
```

Using attributes to define routes clarifies how requests are directed within the application.

4. Ensure Input Validation

Input validation is critical at the controller level to prevent improperly formed data from propagating through the system.

Example:

```csharp
[HttpPost]
public IActionResult Create([FromBody] CreateUserModel model)
{
    if (!ModelState.IsValid)
        return BadRequest(ModelState);

    // Process valid model here
}
```

This method ensures that only valid data is processed, using model validation to protect against bad input.

5. Embrace Asynchronous Programming

Incorporating async operations in controllers helps handle I/O-bound tasks more efficiently, improving application scalability.

Example:

```csharp
[HttpGet("{id}")]
public async Task<IActionResult> GetProduct(int id)
{
    var product = await _productService.GetProductByIdAsync(id);
    if (product is null)
        return NotFound();

    return Ok(product);
}
```

This use of **async** and **await** facilitates non-blocking I/O operations, allowing the server to handle other requests concurrently.

6. Centralize Exception Handling

Using middleware or filters for global exception handling in controllers ensures a cleaner and more focused approach to error management.

7. Integrate Adequate Logging

Implement logging within controllers to capture important information and errors, aiding in troubleshooting and monitoring of application health.

8. Enforce Security Measures

Controllers should implement security strategies like authentication and authorization to safeguard sensitive operations.

Example:

```
[Authorize]
public class AdminController : ControllerBase
{
    // Actions that require admin privileges
}
```

This ensures actions within the **AdminController** are protected and accessible only to authenticated users.

Conclusion

Adopting these best practices for controllers in ASP.NET Core applications ensures that they are not only robust and efficient but also easy to maintain and secure. Optimizing controller architecture significantly impacts the overall functionality and quality of the application, making it well-prepared to meet the demands of complex business requirements.

Chapter Five

Request Handling and Responses

Binding data to parameters

In ASP.NET Core, the technique of automatically mapping data from HTTP requests to parameters in controller action methods is known as model binding. This critical feature enhances the development process by streamlining how data is handled within an application, thus allowing developers to maintain clean and efficient controller codes by abstracting data retrieval mechanics.

The Mechanism of Model Binding

Model binding in ASP.NET Core operates by parsing incoming HTTP requests and intelligently assigning data to the parameters of the corresponding action methods. It works by evaluating the incoming request data against the method's parameters based on both name and data type compatibility. If a mismatch in type occurs, model binding will attempt to convert the incoming data into the required format, if possible.

Data Sources for Model Binding

Model binding can extract data from various components of the HTTP request:

- **Route data:** Information embedded directly in the URL path.

- **Query strings:** Data appended to the URL, following the '?' symbol in key-value pairs.

- **Form fields:** Data included in the body of POST requests.

- **Headers:** Data from the HTTP headers of the request.

- **Request body:** Typically JSON or XML content within the body of the request.

Attributes to Control Model Binding

ASP.NET Core offers multiple attributes that dictate or guide how model binding should interpret and bind incoming data:

1. **[FromBody]**: Directs model binding to use the request body for binding, commonly utilized for JSON or XML payloads.

2. **[FromForm]**: Indicates binding should occur from form data in the POST request body.

3. **[FromQuery]**: Designates that the parameter should be filled from the query string of the request.

4. **[FromRoute]**: Specifies that a parameter should be populated from route data.

5. **[FromHeader]**: Instructs model binding to source the parameter from specific request headers.

Practical Examples of Binding Attributes

Let's examine practical implementations to better understand these concepts:

Example 1: Query String Binding

```csharp
public IActionResult Search([FromQuery] string keyword)
{
    // Logic to process search based on 'keyword'
    return View();
}
```

This function pulls the **keyword** parameter from the request's query string to facilitate a search operation.

Example 2: Route Data Binding

```csharp
[HttpGet("users/{id}")]
public IActionResult GetUser([FromRoute] int id)
{
    // Logic to retrieve and return user details
    return Ok();
}
```

Here, the **id** parameter is populated from the route data of the URL.

Example 3: JSON Body Binding

```csharp
[HttpPost]
public IActionResult UpdateUser([FromBody] UserUpdateModel model)
{
    // Logic to update user information
    return Ok();
}
```

In this instance, **model** is bound using JSON data provided in the body of the POST request.

Best Practices in Model Binding

- **Specify data sources**: Clearly define where each parameter should be bound from using the appropriate attributes to prevent confusion and enhance security.

- **Validate incoming data**: Always verify **ModelState.IsValid** to ensure incoming data adheres to defined validation rules before proceeding with processing.

- **Guard against over-posting**: To prevent over-posting vulnerabilities, use specifically designed view models or DTOs that only include the properties that should be updated.

- **Protect sensitive data**: Utilize attributes like **[BindNever]** to block binding to certain sensitive model properties to safeguard critical data.

Conclusion

Model binding is a vital aspect of ASP.NET Core that facilitates the efficient and effective processing of incoming data into controller actions. By leveraging specific binding attributes and adhering to best practices, developers can enhance the security and robustness of their web applications, ensuring that data is not only correctly parsed and utilized but also protected from common vulnerabilities.

Validating requests

In ASP.NET Core, ensuring that incoming requests are properly validated is a key practice for safeguarding applications from invalid data and potential security threats. Effective request validation helps maintain data integrity, enhances security measures, and improves the overall user interaction with the application. This discussion delves into why request validation is essential and how it can be implemented effectively using ASP.NET Core's capabilities, supplemented by practical examples.

The Necessity of Request Validation

Validating incoming data in web applications is critical for several reasons:

- **Enhancing Security**: It guards against common vulnerabilities such as SQL injections and XSS attacks by ensuring only expected and formatted data is processed.

- **Preserving Data Integrity**: Validation ensures that the data conforms to the defined schema and business rules, reducing processing errors.

- **Improving User Experience**: It allows for the provision of immediate, actionable feedback to users, helping them correct inputs without frustration.

Strategies for Request Validation in ASP.NET Core

ASP.NET Core provides several mechanisms and tools to facilitate robust data validation:

1. **Data Annotations** These are attributes used to decorate model properties, defining intrinsic validation rules that are straightforward to implement.

Example:

```csharp
public class Product
{
    [Required]
    [StringLength(100, MinimumLength = 3)]
    public string Name { get; set; }

    [Range(1, 10000)]
    public decimal Price { get; set; }

    [RegularExpression(@"^[A-Z]+[a-zA-Z]*$")]
    public string Category { get; set; }
}
```

Here, the **Product** class uses data annotations to ensure the name is non-empty and within specific length bounds, the price is within a given range, and the category matches a pattern.

2. **Fluent Validation** This is a third-party library offering a more dynamic and complex validation framework, allowing for the definition of validation rules in a separate, fluent API style.

Example:

```csharp
public class ProductValidator : AbstractValidator<Product>
{
    public ProductValidator()
    {
        RuleFor(x => x.Name).NotEmpty().Length(3, 100);
        RuleFor(x => x.Price).InclusiveBetween(1, 10000);
        RuleFor(x => x.Category).Matches(@"^[A-Z]+[a-zA-Z]*$");
    }
}
```

This setup creates a separate validator for the **Product** model, clearly defining how each field should be validated.

3. **Input Sanitization** This process involves cleaning up the data to remove or encode potentially harmful data elements, especially when the input will interact with a database or be rendered in a browser.

4. **Custom Validation Techniques** For validations that require specific business logic that can't be captured by standard validation tools, custom validation methods can be implemented.

Example:

```csharp
public IActionResult CreateProduct(Product product)
{
    if (!CustomValidateProduct(product))
    {
        return BadRequest("Validation failed");
    }

    // Proceed with saving product
}
```

```
private bool CustomValidateProduct(Product product)
{
    // Custom validation logic here
    return product.Price > 0 && !string.IsNullOrEmpty(product.Name);
}
```

In this example, a custom validation function is used to add additional checks before processing the product.

Best Practices for Validating Requests

- **Validate at the Earliest**: Implement validation as soon as the data enters the application to prevent any corrupted data from moving deeper into the system.

- **Employ a Layered Approach**: Combine different validation strategies to cover all bases—from data annotations for basic checks to custom methods for complex rules.

- **Provide Constructive Feedback**: Ensure that error messages are specific and helpful, guiding users to easily correct mistakes.

- **Separate Validation from Business Logic**: Keep validation logic decoupled from business processes to maintain clean and modular code.

Conclusion

Request validation is an indispensable component of developing secure and reliable ASP.NET Core applications. By using ASP.NET Core's built-in features, along with powerful third-party tools and custom methods, developers can ensure that their applications robustly handle only valid, clean, and intended data. Implementing thorough validation strategies not only prevents security breaches but also significantly enhances the user's interaction with the application.

Producing responses

In ASP.NET Core, effectively managing how responses are crafted and delivered to client requests is critical for building high-performance web applications. Properly structured responses can significantly enhance user interaction and system efficiency. This discussion provides an in-depth look at the techniques for generating responses in ASP.NET Core, offering detailed examples to guide best practices.

Fundamentals of HTTP Responses

Every HTTP request processed by a web server requires a response. These responses can range from delivering HTML content, appropriate for MVC applications, to providing JSON for RESTful APIs. Each response includes necessary data and metadata such as HTTP headers and status codes, which provide crucial information about the response status and how the client should handle it.

Key Response Types in ASP.NET Core

ASP.NET Core facilitates various built-in mechanisms to manage different types of responses, catering to the needs of diverse applications:

1. **View Results**: Mainly used to return HTML content by rendering views. This involves combining view templates with model data to produce dynamic HTML pages.

Example:

```csharp
public IActionResult Index()
{
    var model = _repository.GetItems();
    return View(model);
}
```

Here, the method returns a view by rendering HTML content using the **Index** view template populated with data.

2. **Status Code Results**: These are crucial for communicating the outcome of request processing through HTTP status codes like **200 OK**, **404 Not Found**, or **500 Internal Server Error**.

Example:

```csharp
public IActionResult Delete(int id)
{
    var success = _repository.DeleteItem(id);
    if (!success)
        return NotFound();  // Sends a 404 Not Found

    return NoContent();  // Sends a 204 No Content
}
```

3. **Content Results**: Suitable for returning straightforward text responses directly to the client.

Example:

```csharp
public IActionResult GetServerTime()
{
    return Content(DateTime.Now.ToString());
}
```

4. **JSON Results**: Especially useful in APIs, this format is used to send structured data back to clients, making it ideal for systems that require interoperability.

Example:

```
public IActionResult GetUserDetails(int id)
{
    var user = _userRepository.GetById(id);
    if (user == null)
        return NotFound();

    return Json(user);
}
```

5. **File Results**: Facilitates sending files to clients, whether they are static resources or dynamically generated documents.

Example:

```
public IActionResult DownloadReport(int id)
{
    var reportBytes = _reportService.GenerateReport(id);
    return File(reportBytes, "application/pdf", "report.pdf");
}
```

Best Practices for Response Generation

- **Ensure Proper HTTP Status Codes**: Choosing the correct HTTP status codes is crucial for accurately describing the response and aiding client-side processing.

- **Leverage ASP.NET Core's Action Results**: Make full use of the framework's action results to clarify the intent and make the response handling code more intuitive and maintainable.

- **Content Negotiation**: In API development, manage different response formats effectively to accommodate client preferences and requirements.

- **Manage Response Size**: In scenarios where bandwidth is a concern, optimize response payloads using techniques like compression, pagination, or selective data inclusion.

- **Utilize Caching**: Implement caching strategies for static or infrequently changing data to improve response times and reduce server load.

Conclusion

Understanding and implementing response handling strategies in ASP.NET Core is essential for developers looking to enhance application performance and reliability. By effectively using ASP.NET Core's response generation capabilities, developers can ensure that their applications are robust, responsive, and capable of meeting the demands of varied client requests. This not only improves the user experience but also optimizes system resources.

Content negotiation and media types

Content negotiation is a pivotal technique in web application development, particularly in the creation of APIs with ASP.NET Core. This approach enables a server to deliver various versions of a resource at the same URL, tailored to suit different client preferences based on HTTP request headers. This functionality enhances the API's adaptability and broadens its usability across different client systems by supporting multiple data formats.

The Role of Content Negotiation

Content negotiation utilizes HTTP headers to select the optimal response format for the client. Key headers involved in this process include **Accept**, **Accept-Charset**, **Accept-Encoding**, and **Accept-Language**.

- **Accept**: Determines which media types the client is willing to receive, for example, **application/json** or **application/xml**.

- **Accept-Charset**: Indicates the character sets supported by the client, such as **UTF-8**.

- **Accept-Encoding**: Lists the encoding formats acceptable to the client, like **gzip**, which can optimize data transfer.

- **Accept-Language**: Specifies the client's preferred languages, aiding in delivering localized content.

Managing Media Types in ASP.NET Core

Media types, also known as MIME types, categorize the format of content transmitted over the internet. ASP.NET Core handles these media types efficiently to ensure that responses meet the expected standards set by client requests.

How to Implement Content Negotiation in ASP.NET Core

ASP.NET Core includes native support for content negotiation, allowing for flexible configuration tailored to the needs of the application. By default, it uses the **Accept** header to determine the response format, falling back to a default (typically JSON) when the header is absent.

Configuring MVC to Support Various Formats

To enable your ASP.NET Core application to support different formats such as XML and JSON, you need to configure MVC services to include XML serializers alongside JSON.

Example:

```csharp
public void ConfigureServices(IServiceCollection services)
{
    services.AddControllers()
        .AddNewtonsoftJson()
        .AddXmlSerializerFormatters(); // Activate XML support
}
```

In controller actions, you don't need to specify the response type explicitly; the framework manages content negotiation automatically based on the **Accept** header.

Example:

```csharp
[HttpGet]
public IActionResult Get()
{
    var data = new { Name = "Jane Doe", Age = 28 };
    return Ok(data); // Returns data in JSON or XML, depending on the Accept header
}
```

Best Practices for Content Negotiation

- **Ensure a Default Response Format**: Always set a default format to ensure consistent behavior when the **Accept** header is not provided by the client.

- **Validate Media Types**: Check that the **Accept** header values match supported media types and return a **406 Not Acceptable** status if they do not.

- **Document Supported Formats**: Transparently document which media types your API supports to inform and guide client developers.

- **Use Custom Media Types for API Versioning**: Implement custom media types like **application/vnd.yourapi.v1+json** to manage different versions of your API without changing URLs.

- **Robust Error Handling**: Implement effective error handling to manage cases where content negotiation fails.

Conclusion

Implementing content negotiation in ASP.NET Core APIs significantly enhances their flexibility and client compatibility by dynamically adjusting responses based on client requests. By mastering effective content negotiation techniques, developers can ensure their web applications are versatile and capable of meeting diverse client demands, ultimately leading to more robust and user-friendly solutions.

Chapter Six

Middleware in ASP.NET Core

What is middleware?

Middleware is a critical concept in web development, especially prominent in frameworks like ASP.NET Core. It consists of software components that are configured in a sequence to handle and process HTTP requests and responses within an application. Each piece of middleware can manipulate, pass on, or terminate the request based on specific conditions or requirements. This modular approach is essential for efficiently managing various tasks such as authentication, logging, error handling, and more.

Overview of Middleware in ASP.NET Core

In the ASP.NET Core framework, middleware components are fundamental in constructing the application's request pipeline. This pipeline dictates how requests are handled and responses are issued. Middleware can perform numerous functions including:

- Routing requests to the correct controllers.

- Authenticating users before processing requests.

- Managing errors and exceptions seamlessly across the application.

- Logging request and response data for diagnostics and monitoring.

- Handling sessions and maintaining state information across requests.

Middleware's ability to be chained or ordered allows for a highly customizable request handling process, where each component handles specific aspects of the request and response lifecycle.

How Middleware Operates

Middleware components in ASP.NET Core are typically configured in the **Startup** class's **Configure** method using an **IApplicationBuilder** instance. This setup defines the sequence and conditions under which requests are processed and responses are returned.

Example of Setting Up Middleware:

```
public void Configure(IApplicationBuilder app, IWebHostEnvironment env)
{
    if (env.IsDevelopment())
    {
        app.UseDeveloperExceptionPage();
    }
    else
    {
        app.UseExceptionHandler("/Home/Error");
    }

    app.UseStaticFiles();

    app.UseRouting();

    app.UseAuthorization();
```

```
app.UseEndpoints(endpoints =>
{
    endpoints.MapControllerRoute(
        name: "default",
        pattern: "{controller=Home}/{action=Index}/{id?}");
});
}
```

This configuration script exemplifies the addition of various middleware such as error handling, static file serving, routing, authorization, and endpoint mapping.

Execution Order and Importance

The sequence in which middleware components are added in the Configure method is critical because it determines the order of their execution on incoming requests and their subsequent responses. This order is vital for functionality like authentication, which must be executed before any resource-specific actions are taken.

Creating Custom Middleware

While ASP.NET Core offers a range of built-in middleware, developers also have the flexibility to create their own custom middleware for specific functionalities unique to their applications.

Example of Custom Middleware Implementation:

```csharp
public class MyCustomMiddleware
{
    private readonly RequestDelegate _next;

    public MyCustomMiddleware(RequestDelegate next)
    {
        _next = next;
    }

    public async Task Invoke(HttpContext context)
    {
        // Custom logic before the next middleware
        await _next(context);
        // Custom logic after the next middleware
    }
}
// Extension method to add the middleware
public static class MyCustomMiddlewareExtensions
{
    public static IApplicationBuilder UseMyCustomMiddleware(this
        IApplicationBuilder builder)
    {
        return builder.UseMiddleware<MyCustomMiddleware>();
    }
}
```

This middleware can be integrated into the pipeline with:

```csharp
app.UseMyCustomMiddleware();
```

Conclusion

Middleware in ASP.NET Core is a powerful tool for managing the flow of HTTP requests and responses through a web application. By harnessing and customizing middleware, developers can ensure that their applications handle processes efficiently and securely, leading to robust, maintainable, and effective web applications. Whether utilizing built-in options or crafting bespoke components, middleware is an indispensable asset in modern web application architecture.

Built-in middleware components

In ASP.NET Core, middleware components are essential for orchestrating the handling of HTTP requests and responses within an application's lifecycle. These components are integral to building efficient, secure, and responsive web applications by managing tasks ranging from routing and authentication to error handling.

Exploring Built-in Middleware Components in ASP.NET Core

Middleware in ASP.NET Core serves to facilitate the sequence of operations involved in processing HTTP requests. Each component in the middleware pipeline can alter or halt the request, or pass it down the pipeline for further processing. Below are some critical built-in middleware components provided by ASP.NET Core:

1. **Authentication Middleware (UseAuthentication)**: This middleware authenticates users, crucial for applications that restrict access based on user identity.

Example:

```
public void Configure(IApplicationBuilder app)
{
    app.UseAuthentication();
}
```

2. **Authorization Middleware (UseAuthorization)**: Complementing the Authentication Middleware, this component enforces security policies to ensure that users have the necessary permissions to access resources.

Example:

```
public void Configure(IApplicationBuilder app)
{
    app.UseAuthentication();
    app.UseAuthorization();
}
```

3. **Static Files Middleware (UseStaticFiles)**: This middleware handles requests for static files, such as images, JavaScript, and CSS files, from the application's web root directory.

Example:

```
public void Configure(IApplicationBuilder app)
{
    app.UseStaticFiles(); // Enables static file serving
}
```

4. **Routing Middleware (UseRouting)**: Essential for matching incoming requests to appropriate routes and handlers, facilitating the correct dispatch of requests within the application.

Example:

```
public void Configure(IApplicationBuilder app)
{
    app.UseRouting();
}
```

5. **Session Middleware (UseSession)**: This middleware allows for the management of user sessions, helping preserve data across multiple requests from the same client.

Example:

```
public void Configure(IApplicationBuilder app)
{
    app.UseSession();
}
```

6. **MVC Middleware (UseEndpoints)**: Configures endpoints for MVC controllers or Razor Pages, ensuring that requests are processed by the correct resources.

Example:

```
public void Configure(IApplicationBuilder app)
{
    app.UseRouting();

    app.UseEndpoints(endpoints =>
    {
        endpoints.MapControllerRoute(
            name: "default",
            pattern: "{controller=Home}/{action=Index}/{id?}");
    });
}
```

7. **Exception Handling Middleware (UseDeveloperExceptionPage and UseExceptionHandler)**: Provides mechanisms for handling exceptions across the application. **UseDeveloperExceptionPage** offers detailed error information useful in development, while

UseExceptionHandler routes errors to a specified path in production environments.

Example:

```
public void Configure(IApplicationBuilder app, IWebHostEnvironment env)
{
    if (env.IsDevelopment())
    {
        app.UseDeveloperExceptionPage();
    }
    else
    {
        app.UseExceptionHandler("/Home/Error");
    }
}
```

Best Practices for Employing Built-in Middleware

- **Ordering is Key**: The sequence in which middleware components are configured significantly impacts their effectiveness in processing requests and responses.

- **Secure Configuration is Essential**: Properly set up middleware that handles sensitive operations, such as authentication and authorization, to safeguard against vulnerabilities.

- **Adjust for Environments**: Configure middleware behavior conditionally based on the development or production environment to optimize both development flexibility and production security.

Conclusion

Built-in middleware components in ASP.NET Core provide a structured approach to handling various aspects of HTTP request processing, enabling developers to build sophisticated web applications. By judiciously configuring these middleware components, developers can ensure their applications are well-equipped to handle modern web demands efficiently and securely.

Creating custom middleware

In ASP.NET Core, custom middleware acts as a vital mechanism for inserting tailored processing logic into the HTTP request pipeline. This customization is critical for addressing specific behaviors and requirements not covered by standard middleware, such as advanced logging, detailed error management, or unique request handling strategies.

Concept of Custom Middleware in ASP.NET Core

Custom middleware components are user-defined elements that integrate seamlessly into ASP.NET Core's request processing chain. These components allow developers to execute specific actions on HTTP requests and responses, enhancing the application's functionality and responsiveness.

Developing Custom Middleware

Implementing custom middleware involves several key steps, from creating the middleware class to deploying it within the application's pipeline:

1. **Crafting the Middleware Class**: The foundation of custom middleware is a class that encapsulates the desired functionality. This class typically includes a constructor that accepts a **RequestDelegate** (which

points to the next middleware component) and methods that define the middleware's operations.

Example:

```
public class CustomLoggingMiddleware
{
    private readonly RequestDelegate _next;
    private readonly ILogger _logger;

    public CustomLoggingMiddleware(RequestDelegate next, ILogger
        <CustomLoggingMiddleware> logger)
    {
        _next = next;
        _logger = logger;
    }

    public async Task InvokeAsync(HttpContext context)
    {
        _logger.LogInformation("Handling request: " + context.Request.Path);
        await _next(context);
        _logger.LogInformation("Request has been processed.");
    }
}
```

This example demonstrates a middleware that logs details about each request before and after it is processed, providing valuable insights for debugging and monitoring.

2. **Extension Method for Middleware Registration**: To simplify the integration of the middleware into the application's pipeline, an extension method is typically created. This method makes it easier to add the middleware using a fluent configuration style.

Example:

```
public static class CustomLoggingMiddlewareExtensions
{
    public static IApplicationBuilder UseCustomLogging(this IApplicationBuilder
        builder)
    {
        return builder.UseMiddleware<CustomLoggingMiddleware>();
    }
}
```

3. **Incorporating the Middleware into the Pipeline**: The middleware is activated by including it in the **Configure** method of the **Startup** class, ensuring it is part of the request processing sequence.

Example:

```
public void Configure(IApplicationBuilder app, IWebHostEnvironment env)
{
    if (env.IsDevelopment())
    {
        app.UseDeveloperExceptionPage();
    }

    app.UseCustomLogging();

    app.UseRouting();
    app.UseAuthorization();
    app.UseEndpoints(endpoints =>
    {
        endpoints.MapControllers();
    });
}
```

In this configuration, the custom logging middleware is strategically placed to log information about requests post-initial error handling and prior to routing.

Best Practices for Custom Middleware Development

- **Handle Exceptions Effectively**: It's essential that your middleware manages exceptions efficiently to maintain the integrity of the middleware pipeline.

- **Leverage Asynchronous Programming**: Opt for async/await patterns in your middleware to enhance application performance and avoid blocking critical threads.

- **Thorough Testing**: Due to its integral role in request processing, it's crucial to test middleware extensively across different scenarios to ensure it performs reliably and interacts correctly with other components.

Conclusion

Creating custom middleware in ASP.NET Core enables developers to enhance their applications with specific functionalities tailored to their unique processing needs. By understanding how to effectively implement and integrate custom middleware, developers can take full advantage of ASP.NET Core's flexible architecture to build sophisticated, well-optimized web applications.

Configuring middleware pipeline

In ASP.NET Core, the middleware pipeline plays a crucial role in determining how HTTP requests are processed within an application. Each middleware component within this pipeline has the responsibility to either pass the request along to the next component, perform specific actions before or after the next component, or stop further processing. Configuring this pipeline effectively is vital for building robust, secure, and efficient web applications. This discussion provides insights into how to configure the middleware pipeline, emphasizing the importance of strategic setup and adherence to best practices.

Configuring the Middleware Pipeline in ASP.NET Core

Middleware configuration is primarily handled in the **Startup** class of an ASP.NET Core application, particularly within the **Configure** method. This method utilizes the **IApplicationBuilder** instance, allowing developers to add middleware components to the pipeline in the desired order.

Here's a typical example of how a middleware pipeline might be configured:

```csharp
public void Configure(IApplicationBuilder app, IWebHostEnvironment env)
{
    if (env.IsDevelopment())
    {
        app.UseDeveloperExceptionPage(); // Provides detailed error information in development
    }
    else
    {
        app.UseExceptionHandler("/Home/Error"); // Redirects to an error page
        app.UseHsts(); // Enforces strict transport security
    }

    app.UseHttpsRedirection(); // Redirects HTTP requests to HTTPS
    app.UseStaticFiles(); // Handles requests for static files

    app.UseRouting(); // Enables routing capabilities

    app.UseAuthentication(); // Manages user authentication
    app.UseAuthorization(); // Handles authorization based on authenticated user
```

```
app.UseEndpoints(endpoints =>
{
    endpoints.MapControllers(); // Maps incoming requests to controller
        actions
    endpoints.MapRazorPages(); // Maps requests to Razor Pages
});
}
```

Critical Components in the Middleware Pipeline

1. Exception Handling: Implement **UseDeveloperExceptionPage** or **UseExceptionHandler** early in the pipeline to catch and handle exceptions effectively.

2. Security Enhancements: Utilize **UseHttpsRedirection** and **UseHsts** to improve security by enforcing HTTPS connections.

3. Static Files: Configure **UseStaticFiles** to efficiently serve static resources such as images, CSS files, and JavaScript.

4. Core Request Handling: Insert **UseRouting**, **UseAuthentication**, and **UseAuthorization** at strategic points to ensure correct routing and secure access to resources.

5. Endpoint Configuration: Use **UseEndpoints** to define how requests are mapped to actions or pages within the application.

Best Practices for Middleware Configuration

Consider the Order of Middleware: The sequence in which middleware components are added is crucial, as it affects their execution and the overall response behavior. For example, authentication should generally precede any middleware that requires user information.

Adapt Configuration for Different Environments: Tailor middleware settings based on the application's environment (development, production, etc.), utilizing conditional logic to optimize functionality and security for each scenario.

Minimize Custom Middleware Usage: While custom middleware offers flexibility, it should be used selectively to avoid complexity. Rely on built-in middleware whenever possible and ensure any custom middleware is well-documented and thoroughly tested.

Comprehensive Testing: Given middleware's significant role in application functionality, both unit and integration testing are essential. These tests help ensure that each piece of middleware performs as expected and that the entire pipeline operates seamlessly.

Conclusion

Effective configuration of the middleware pipeline is essential for leveraging ASP.NET Core's full potential in handling HTTP requests. By understanding the roles and proper setup of various middleware components and observing best practices for their configuration, developers can create applications that are not only functional but also secure, performant, and easy to maintain. This structured approach to middleware configuration helps maintain clarity in application behavior and enhances overall system robustness.

Chapter Seven

Managing Dependencies

Understanding dependency injection

Dependency Injection (DI) is a critical design pattern in contemporary software engineering, widely adopted for managing the dependencies between objects. This pattern is particularly pivotal in .NET development and forms a core part of frameworks like ASP.NET Core. It facilitates more maintainable, testable, and modular software by decoupling the components of an application.

Understanding Dependency Injection

Dependency Injection is a method where an object obtains its dependencies from an external source rather than constructing them internally. This approach minimizes the coupling between components, making the software easier to manage and adapt to changes.

The key roles involved in DI are:

- **The Client**: The object that requires the dependency.
- **The Interface**: Defines the communication between the dependency and the client.
- **The Injector**: Creates and provides the dependency to the client.

Advantages of Dependency Injection

1. **Minimized Coupling**: DI reduces dependencies between components, allowing for easier management and updates.

2. **Enhanced Flexibility**: Changes to dependencies or their implementations do not impact dependent classes, facilitating easier updates and maintenance.

3. **Improved Testability**: DI makes it simpler to replace real dependencies with mock ones during testing, enhancing test coverage and simplicity.

4. **Simplified Management**: As applications grow, managing component creation and dependencies becomes more straightforward with DI.

Implementing Dependency Injection in ASP.NET Core

ASP.NET Core includes built-in support for dependency injection, offering a comprehensive service container that can inject dependencies automatically through constructors.

Here's how to implement DI in ASP.NET Core:

1. Define an Interface

Start by defining an interface that outlines the expected functionalities of the dependency:

```
public interface IGreetingService
{
    string Greet(string name);
}
```

2. Implement the Interface

Create a class that implements this interface:

```csharp
public class GreetingService : IGreetingService
{
    public string Greet(string name)
    {
        return $"Hello, {name}!";
    }
}
```

3. Configure Services

Within the **Startup.cs** of your ASP.NET Core application, configure the DI container to use your service:

```csharp
public void ConfigureServices(IServiceCollection services)
{
    services.AddScoped<IGreetingService, GreetingService>();
}
```

AddScoped is used here, indicating that a new instance of GreetingService will be created for each request.

4. Injecting the Dependency

Inject the service into the constructors of the classes that need it, such as controllers:

```csharp
public class HomeController : Controller
{
    private readonly IGreetingService _greetingService;

    public HomeController(IGreetingService greetingService)
    {
        _greetingService = greetingService;
    }

    public IActionResult Index()
    {
        var greeting = _greetingService.Greet("World");
        return Content(greeting);
    }
}
```

In this setup, **HomeController** receives an **IGreetingService**, with ASP.NET Core's DI container handling the instantiation of **GreetingService**.

Dependency Injection Scopes

ASP.NET Core defines several lifetimes for services in the DI container:

- **Transient**: Each request for a service results in a new instance.
- **Scoped**: A single instance is created for each request.
- **Singleton**: A single instance is created and used throughout the application's lifetime.

The choice of lifetime should align with the service's required usage and design considerations.

Conclusion

Dependency Injection enhances the scalability, robustness, and testability of applications by ensuring components remain loosely coupled and management-friendly. In ASP.NET Core, leveraging DI effectively allows developers to build dynamic, efficient applications poised for growth and adaptability. This architectural strategy supports better development practices and can significantly improve both application performance and developer productivity.

Setting up and using services

In ASP.NET Core, effectively managing and utilizing services is paramount for constructing maintainable and scalable applications. Services, in this context, are discrete units of functionality encapsulated within classes, such as logging mechanisms, data access operations, or business logic processors. These are configured to be reusable across the application, fostering a more modular and testable codebase. This exploration delves into how to properly configure and utilize services in ASP.NET Core, highlighting the role of dependency injection in facilitating this process.

Overview of Services in ASP.NET Core

Services in ASP.NET Core are typically components abstracted into classes that handle specific functionalities like interaction with databases, external services, or complex business operations. These services are registered with ASP.NET Core's built-in dependency injection container, which then provides these services wherever they are needed within the application.

Configuring Services

Configuring services in an ASP.NET Core application generally takes place in the **Startup** class. This involves registering each service with a specific lifecycle depending on how they are used within the application.

1. **Service Registration**: Services are registered in the **ConfigureServices** method of the **Startup** class. This is where you define how services are created, like transient, scoped, or singleton.

Here's how you might register services:

```
public void ConfigureServices(IServiceCollection services)
{
    // Registering a data access service with scoped lifetime
    services.AddScoped<IDataRepository, DataRepository>();

    // Registering a logging service with singleton lifetime
    services.AddSingleton<ILogger, Logger>();
}
```

In the above example:

- **IDataRepository** is registered as scoped, meaning a new instance is created for each request.

- **ILogger** is registered as a singleton, persisting as a single instance across the application's lifetime.

2. **Service Consumption**: Once services are registered, they can be injected into any part of the application that the framework manages, such as controllers or other services. Dependency injection automates the process of providing the registered services where needed.

Example of injecting a service into a controller:

```csharp
public class ProductsController : Controller
{
    private readonly IDataRepository _repository;

    public ProductsController(IDataRepository repository)
    {
        _repository = repository;
    }

    public IActionResult List()
    {
        var products = _repository.GetAllProducts();
        return View(products);
    }
}
```

Best Practices in Service Usage

1. **Interface-Based Definitions**: Implement services based on interfaces to decouple the actual implementation from the usage, enhancing modifiability and testability. This makes it easier to replace implementations without affecting consumers.

2. **Appropriate Service Lifetimes**:
    - **Transient**: Best for lightweight and stateless services.
    - **Scoped**: Suitable for services that need to preserve state within a request.
    - **Singleton**: Optimal for services that are expensive to create or must share data across the application.
3. **Avoid Using Service Locator Pattern**: Instead of fetching services on demand using a service locator, rely on dependency injection to provide necessary dependencies, which simplifies code and reduces errors.
4. **Ensure Services Are Testable**: Design services with testing in mind by limiting responsibilities and using interfaces. This approach allows for easy substitution of services with mock objects during testing, facilitating more effective unit tests.

Conclusion

Configuring and using services correctly in ASP.NET Core is crucial for building efficient, robust, and scalable applications. By adhering to the principles of dependency injection, developers can ensure a clean separation of concerns and a more manageable codebase. Proper service setup and utilization lead to applications that are easier to maintain and extend, aligning with best practices for enterprise-grade software development.

Lifetime and registration options

In ASP.NET Core, the management of service lifetimes and registration options plays a critical role in ensuring that applications run efficiently, maintain scalability, and uphold robust architecture. Understanding how services are instantiated and managed throughout the application's lifecycle is key to optimizing performance, ensuring appropriate resource use, and achieving clean and maintainable code.

Exploring Service Lifetimes

ASP.NET Core's dependency injection (DI) framework supports multiple lifetimes for services, each designed for different scenarios:

1. **Transient**

    - **Overview**: Transient services are created anew with each request from the service container. This lifetime is typically used for lightweight, stateless services.

    - **Applicability**: Best used for services that do not retain information between requests.

    - **Code Example**:

```
services.AddTransient<IEmailService, EmailService>();
```

2. **Scoped**
    - **Overview**: Scoped services are instantiated once per client request, meaning a new instance is created for each HTTP request.
    - **Applicability**: Ideal for services that need to preserve information within a request but not beyond that.
    - **Code Example**:

```
services.AddScoped<IUserSession, UserSession>();
```

3. **Singleton**
    - **Overview**: Singleton services are created the first time they are requested or when services are configured during application startup. This same instance is then used across all subsequent requests.
    - **Applicability**: Suitable for services that require expensive resources or need to maintain state shared across the application.
    - **Code Example**:

```
services.AddSingleton<ICacheProvider, CacheProvider>();
```

Service Registration Techniques

ASP.NET Core offers diverse options for registering services, providing flexibility in how dependencies are configured:

1. **Instance Registration**
    - **Usage**: Directly registering a pre-constructed instance of a service can be particularly useful when integrating with external libraries or shared instances created outside of ASP.NET Core's DI container.
    - **Example**:

```
var settings = new AppSettings();
services.AddSingleton(settings);
```

2. **Factory-Based Registration**
    - **Usage**: For complex creation scenarios requiring custom logic, services can be instantiated via a factory method. This is especially useful when service creation involves dependencies themselves.
    - **Example**:

```
services.AddTransient<IMyDependency, MyDependency>(provider =>
{
    var dependency = provider.GetRequiredService<IOtherDependency>();
    return new MyDependency(dependency);
});
```

3. **Conditional Registration**
    - **Usage**: Useful for registering a service only if it hasn't been registered previously or when different implementations are needed based on specific conditions.

- Example:

```
services.TryAddSingleton<ILogger, Logger>();
```

Best Practices for Service Lifetime and Registration

1. **Recognize Dependency Relationships**: Mismanaged service lifetimes, like a singleton depending on a scoped service, can lead to issues like captive dependencies and memory leaks.

2. **Prefer Shorter Lifetimes When Possible**: Transient and scoped services generally pose fewer risks compared to singletons, which can retain state and resources longer than needed.

3. **Limit Use of Factory Functions**: While factory functions offer great control, they can complicate the service configuration landscape if not used judiciously.

4. **Handle Object Disposal Carefully**: Ensure that services which implement **IDisposable** are correctly managed by the DI container or manually disposed of to avoid resource leaks.

5. **Incorporate Comprehensive Testing**: Regularly test and validate configurations, especially in complex scenarios where multiple services interact, to ensure that lifetimes and registrations are correct and effective.

Conclusion

Effective management of service lifetimes and registration in ASP.NET Core is essential for developing applications that are not only efficient but also easy to maintain and scale. By selecting the right lifetime for each service and employing thoughtful registration strategies, developers can maximize the benefits of ASP.NET Core's DI capabilities, leading to better application performance and sustainability. Understanding these principles deeply empowers developers to construct sophisticated and high-performing web applications.

Dependency injection best practices

Dependency injection (DI) is an essential design pattern that enhances modularity and testability in software development, particularly in frameworks like ASP.NET Core. It involves the technique of providing objects that a class needs (its dependencies) rather than having it construct them internally. By following DI best practices, developers can create software that is easier to manage, maintain, and evolve. This discussion details effective strategies for implementing dependency injection within ASP.NET Core to build robust, maintainable, and scalable applications.

1. Employ Interfaces for Dependency Definitions

Using interfaces to represent dependencies promotes a flexible and decoupled system design. This practice allows developers to substitute different implementations without altering the dependent classes.

Example:

```
public interface IOrderProcessor
{
    void ProcessOrder(Order order);
}
```

```csharp
public class OrderProcessor : IOrderProcessor
{
    public void ProcessOrder(Order order)
    {
        // Implementation code here
    }
}
```

Injecting **IOrderProcessor** rather than a concrete **OrderProcessor** facilitates the easy swapping of the implementation, thereby enhancing maintainability.

2. Explicitly Register Dependencies

In ASP.NET Core, all dependencies should be explicitly registered in the **Startup.ConfigureServices** method, specifying their lifetimes. This not only documents the application's architecture but also governs the behavior of instances throughout the application's lifecycle.

Example:

```csharp
public void ConfigureServices(IServiceCollection services)
{
    services.AddScoped<IProductRepository, ProductRepository>();
    services.AddTransient<IBillingService, BillingService>();
    services.AddSingleton<IApplicationConfiguration, ApplicationConfiguration>();
}
```

Here, different services are registered with appropriate lifetimes (Scoped, Transient, Singleton), affecting instance management and availability.

3. Avoid Captive Dependencies

It's crucial to manage dependency lifetimes wisely to prevent captive dependencies, where longer-lived services mistakenly depend on shorter-lived ones.

Example:

```
// Incorrect
services.AddSingleton<IUserContext, UserContext>(); // Scoped expected
services.AddScoped<IRepository, UserRepository>();

// Correct
services.AddScoped<IUserContext, UserContext>();
services.AddScoped<IRepository, UserRepository>();
```

4. Prefer Constructor Injection

Constructor injection is preferred for its clarity and the immutability it confers on the injected service. It ensures that an object cannot exist without its dependencies being properly initialized.

Example:

```
public class AccountService : IAccountService
{
    private readonly IAccountRepository _repository;

    public AccountService(IAccountRepository repository)
    {
        _repository = repository;
    }
}
```

This pattern forces the provision of an **IAccountRepository** when **AccountService** is instantiated, guaranteeing that the service is always in a valid state.

5. Maintain Readability and Simplicity

While dependency injection is powerful, overuse or misuse can complicate the codebase unnecessarily. Maintain simplicity and prioritize readability when applying DI principles.

Example:

```csharp
// Questionable use
public class UtilityService
{
    private readonly IComplexDependency _complexDependency;

    public UtilityService(IComplexDependency complexDependency)
    {
        _complexDependency = complexDependency;
    }

    public void SimpleAction()
    {
        _complexDependency.SimpleMethod();
        // Reconsider if DI is necessary for simple, minimal methods
    }
}
```

In situations where the dependency is overly complex for the task, consider simpler approaches like direct method calls or static utilities.

6. Design with Testability in Mind

Design services to be easily testable by abstracting dependencies through interfaces and avoiding static methods or singletons that carry state.

Example:

```csharp
public interface IEmailClient
{
    bool SendEmail(Message message);
}
public class TestEmailClient : IEmailClient
{
    public bool SendEmail(Message message)
    {
        return true; // Simulated response for testing
    }
}
```

Using mock implementations like **TestEmailClient** simplifies unit testing by allowing for controlled tests with predictable outputs.

Conclusion

Adopting these best practices for dependency injection in ASP.NET Core can significantly elevate the quality of the software by ensuring that applications are easy to test, maintain, and scale. These strategies enable developers to create systems that are not only efficient but also robust, ensuring longevity and reliability in application performance.

Chapter Eight

Database Connectivity

Overview of Entity Framework Core

Entity Framework Core (EF Core) is a sophisticated and extendable version of Entity Framework, Microsoft's highly-regarded data access technology. As an object-relational mapper (ORM), EF Core allows developers to interact with databases using .NET objects, thereby reducing the amount of boilerplate data access code developers need to write.

Overview of Entity Framework Core

EF Core is an advanced ORM framework that facilitates data interaction within .NET applications through an intuitive API. It supports both Code-First and Database-First development approaches, enhancing its adaptability across different types of applications such as web, desktop, and mobile applications.

This framework simplifies database operations by abstracting complex commands into simple CRUD operations and managing transactional code and change tracking automatically. At runtime, it converts queries written using Language Integrated Query (LINQ) into SQL, providing developers a powerful, strongly-typed method of querying data.

Key Features of Entity Framework Core

1. **LINQ Queries**: EF Core processes queries written in LINQ by transforming them into SQL queries that can be executed against a database, while the results are returned as manageable .NET objects.

2. **Change Tracking**: Automatic monitoring of changes to instances of your entities allows EF Core to generate the necessary SQL commands to update the database when the **SaveChanges()** method is called.

3. **Navigation Properties**: Easily manage relationships such as One-to-Many or Many-to-Many through navigable properties in your entity classes.

4. **Migrations**: EF Core's migrations support helps developers to iteratively apply changes to the database to keep it synchronized with the application's data model while preserving existing data.

5. **Transactions**: EF Core provides built-in transaction support essential for maintaining data integrity, especially during operations that modify multiple tables.

6. **Caching**: It improves the performance of applications by caching the results of queries, reducing the need to repeatedly query the database for the same data.

7. **Concurrency Control**: EF Core uses optimistic concurrency control to handle situations where multiple transactions might attempt to update the same data concurrently.

Getting Started with Entity Framework Core

To begin using EF Core, it's necessary to install the appropriate NuGet package for the database provider you're using. EF Core supports a wide range of databases, from SQL Server to PostgreSQL.

```
dotnet add package Microsoft.EntityFrameworkCore.SqlServer
dotnet add package Microsoft.EntityFrameworkCore.Tools
```

Here's a basic setup to illustrate the integration of EF Core in an application:

```
using Microsoft.EntityFrameworkCore;

public class ApplicationContext : DbContext
{
    public DbSet<Article> Articles { get; set; }

    protected override void OnConfiguring(DbContextOptionsBuilder options)
        => options.UseSqlServer(@"Server=(localdb)\mssqllocaldb;Database=MyApp;Integrated Security=True");
}

public class Article
{
    public int ArticleId { get; set; }
    public string Title { get; set; }
}
```

```csharp
class Program
{
    static void Main(string[] args)
    {
        using (var context = new ApplicationContext())
        {
            context.Articles.Add(new Article { Title = "Introduction to EF
                Core" });
            context.SaveChanges();

            var article = context.Articles.First();
            Console.WriteLine($"Article: {article.Title}");
        }
    }
}
```

In this example, **ApplicationContext** manages the database context, including a **DbSet<Article>** to manage articles. The connection string for SQL Server is configured in the **OnConfiguring** method.

Best Practices for Using Entity Framework Core

- **Projection Queries**: Limit queries to retrieve only necessary data fields to reduce data fetch costs.

- **Indexing**: Ensure database columns used in **WHERE**, **ORDER BY**, or **JOIN** conditions are properly indexed.

- **Performance Monitoring**: Continuously monitor and profile SQL queries and overall database performance.

- **Asynchronous API**: Utilize EF Core's asynchronous methods to enhance application performance and responsiveness.

Conclusion

Entity Framework Core streamlines data handling in .NET applications, offering powerful capabilities like automatic change tracking, easy relationship management, and robust migration support. For developers committed to the .NET stack, EF Core provides a comprehensive, efficient, and scalable approach to ORM that integrates seamlessly with various types of applications.

Configuring a database context

In the development landscape of ASP.NET Core and Entity Framework Core (EF Core), properly configuring a database context is essential. This configuration is crucial because it serves as the primary channel through which applications interact with their databases. The **DbContext** in EF Core acts as the orchestrator for these interactions, managing the database connections, handling the operations on the data, and providing a mapping from CLR objects to database records.

Essentials of Database Context in EF Core

A **DbContext** serves as the operational hub for all database-related activities in EF Core, enabling CRUD operations, transaction management, and much more. Here's a detailed walkthrough on how to effectively set up a **DbContext**:

1. **Definition of the DbContext** Begin by defining a class that inherits from **DbContext**. This class will encapsulate the database session and should define

properties of type **DbSet<T>** to represent the entities of your domain model.

Example:

```csharp
public class SchoolContext : DbContext
{
    public DbSet<Student> Students { get; set; }
    public DbSet<Course> Courses { get; set; }
}
```

Student and **Course** are entity classes that correspond to database tables.

2. **Configuration of the DbContext** Override the **OnConfiguring** method in your **DbContext** class to set up the database provider and other necessary configuration options like the connection string.

Example:

```csharp
protected override void OnConfiguring(DbContextOptionsBuilder optionsBuilder)
{
    optionsBuilder.UseSqlServer(@"Server=(localdb)\mssqllocaldb;Database=SchoolDB;Integrated Security=True");
}
```

This snippet configures SQL Server as the database provider.

3. **DbContext Configuration via Dependency Injection** For better modularity and testability, configure your **DbContext** using dependency injection in the **Startup.cs** of your ASP.NET Core application.

Example:

```csharp
public void ConfigureServices(IServiceCollection services)
{
    services.AddDbContext<SchoolContext>(options =>
        options.UseSqlServer(Configuration.GetConnectionString("DefaultConnection")));
}
```

This method pulls the connection string from the **appsettings.json** file, maintaining security and flexibility.

4. **Using the DbContext** Inject the **DbContext** into your controllers or services to utilize it for database operations.

Example:

```csharp
public class StudentsController : Controller
{
    private readonly SchoolContext _context;

    public StudentsController(SchoolContext context)
    {
        context = context;
    }

    public async Task<IActionResult> Index()
    {
        var students = await _context.Students.ToListAsync();
        return View(students);
    }
}
```

Here, **SchoolContext** is injected into **StudentsController**, enabling it to fetch and display students.

Best Practices for Configuring DbContext

- **Maintain DbContext Purity**: Keep your **DbContext** focused strictly on database interactions.

- **Securely Manage Connection Strings**: Never hardcode connection strings in your codebase; instead, use configuration files or environment variables.

- **Control DbContext Lifetime**: Be strategic about the lifecycle management of your **DbContext** instances to avoid performance bottlenecks.

- **Data Access Optimization**: Make informed choices about loading data (lazy, eager, explicit) based on your application's needs.

- **Schema Management Through Migrations**: Use EF Core migrations to handle database schema changes effectively and safely.

Conclusion

Proper configuration of the **DbContext** in an EF Core application is fundamental to building efficient, secure, and maintainable applications. Following the outlined setup and best practices ensures that your application can robustly handle interactions with the database, making it well-suited for both development and high-demand production environments. This approach not only streamlines development efforts but also enhances the overall quality and performance of the application.

Performing CRUD operations

In software development, especially within frameworks like ASP.NET Core, mastering CRUD operations—Create, Read, Update, Delete—is crucial for effective database interaction. These operations enable application users to manage their data efficiently, ensuring applications are dynamic and scalable.

Essentials of CRUD Operations

CRUD operations are vital for database manipulation, allowing for:

- **Create** operations, which add new records to the database.

- **Read** operations, which pull existing data from the database.

- **Update** operations, which alter data in existing database records.

- **Delete** operations, which eliminate records from the database.

These operations are critical across various computing platforms and essential for developers to master.

Implementing CRUD with Entity Framework Core in ASP.NET Core

Entity Framework Core (EF Core) offers a streamlined mechanism for CRUD operations, enhancing data management in ASP.NET Core applications. Here's how you can implement these operations using EF Core:

1. Setup

Start by setting up your ASP.NET Core project with EF Core, including the necessary packages for your database provider (e.g., SQL Server, PostgreSQL).

```
dotnet add package Microsoft.EntityFrameworkCore.SqlServer
dotnet add package Microsoft.EntityFrameworkCore.Design
```

Define your database context and model classes:

```
public class SchoolContext : DbContext
{
    public DbSet<Student> Students { get; set; }

    protected override void OnConfiguring(DbContextOptionsBuilder optionsBuilder)
    {
        optionsBuilder.UseSqlServer("Your_Connection_String");
    }
}
public class Student
{
    public int StudentId { get; set; }
    public string Name { get; set; }
}
```

2. Create Operation

To add new records, instantiate your model, add it to the **DbSet**, and save the changes:

```
using (var context = new SchoolContext())
{
    var student = new Student { Name = "John Doe" };
    context.Students.Add(student);
    context.SaveChanges();
}
```

3. Read Operation

Retrieve data using LINQ to query the **DbSet**:

```csharp
using (var context = new SchoolContext())
{
    var student = context.Students
                        .FirstOrDefault(s => s.StudentId == 1);
    Console.WriteLine(student?.Name);
}
```

4. Update Operation

Update a record by fetching it, changing its properties, and committing the changes:

```csharp
using (var context = new SchoolContext())
{
    var student = context.Students.FirstOrDefault(s => s.StudentId == 1);
    if (student != null)
    {
        student.Name = "Jane Doe";
        context.SaveChanges();
    }
}
```

5. Delete Operation

Delete a record by retrieving it, removing it from the **DbSet**, and saving the changes:

```csharp
using (var context = new SchoolContext())
{
    var student = context.Students.FirstOrDefault(s => s.StudentId == 1);
    if (student != null)
    {
        context.Students.Remove(student);
        context.SaveChanges();
    }
}
```

Best Practices for CRUD Operations

- **Leverage Asynchronous Methods**: Use asynchronous methods like **SaveChangesAsync** and **ToListAsync** to improve responsiveness.

- **Handle Concurrent Data Access**: Implement strategies to manage data concurrency effectively.

- **Validate Data Thoroughly**: Conduct rigorous data validation both client-side and server-side before create or update operations.

- **Implement Robust Error Handling**: Develop comprehensive error handling strategies to manage potential failures gracefully.

- **Optimize Query Performance**: Regularly profile and optimize your queries to enhance performance.

Conclusion

Managing CRUD operations effectively in ASP.NET Core with EF Core is key to building robust, efficient applications. By following best practices and utilizing EF Core's capabilities, developers can ensure that their applications are not only reliable but also maintainable and scalable, providing a solid user experience through efficient data management.

Asynchronous database operations

In today's software development landscape, efficient management of database tasks is crucial for maintaining application performance and scalability. Asynchronous database operations are vital in this regard, facilitating non-blocking interactions with databases, which is especially important in high-traffic environments to ensure smooth operation and effective resource utilization.

Understanding Asynchronous Operations

Asynchronous operations allow applications to initiate database tasks and continue with other operations without waiting for the task completion. This non-blocking behavior is critical for preventing UI freezes and backend slowdowns, enhancing user experience and system efficiency. In the .NET framework, particularly with Entity Framework Core (EF Core), support for asynchronous operations is robust, utilizing the Task-based Asynchronous Pattern (TAP) for optimal implementation.

Benefits of Asynchronous Database Operations

1. **Improved Application Responsiveness**: Asynchronous operations ensure that the application's main execution thread remains unblocked, enhancing user interface responsiveness.

2. **Scalability**: By enabling the system to handle other requests while awaiting database task completions, asynchronous operations significantly aid scalability.

3. **Resource Optimization**: These operations promote better use of server resources, reducing idle times and improving overall efficiency in handling I/O-bound tasks.

Implementing Asynchronous Operations Using EF Core

EF Core supports asynchronous operations through various methods such as **ToListAsync()**, **SaveChangesAsync()**, and **FirstOrDefaultAsync()**. These methods help prevent the main execution thread from being blocked during database access.

Setting Up for Asynchronous Operations

To utilize asynchronous operations in EF Core, ensure your .NET application is properly configured with the necessary EF Core packages and is targeting .NET 4.5 or newer.

Here's an example configuration:

```csharp
public class BusinessContext : DbContext
{
    public DbSet<Product> Products { get; set; }

    protected override void OnConfiguring(DbContextOptionsBuilder optionsBuilder)
    {
        optionsBuilder.UseSqlServer("Your_Connection_String");
    }
}

public class Product
{
    public int ProductId { get; set; }
    public string Description { get; set; }
}
```

Example: Asynchronous CRUD Operations

An example function for asynchronously updating a database record might look like this:

```csharp
public async Task UpdateProductAsync(int productId, string description)
{
    using (var context = new BusinessContext())
    {
        var product = await context.Products.FirstOrDefaultAsync(p => p.ProductId
            == productId);
        if (product != null)
        {
            product.Description = description;
            await context.SaveChangesAsync();
        }
    }
}
```

In this scenario, **FirstOrDefaultAsync** fetches a product asynchronously, and **SaveChangesAsync** commits any modifications, efficiently freeing up the thread when waiting on the database.

Best Practices for Asynchronous Operations

- **Maintain Asynchronous Flow**: Ensure that asynchronous calls are maintained throughout the call stack to avoid potential deadlocks and ensure consistency.

- **Robust Exception Handling**: Asynchronous paths should have comprehensive exception handling mechanisms to address runtime errors gracefully.

- **Appropriate Usage**: Employ asynchronous methods primarily for I/O-bound operations, not CPU-bound tasks, to optimize their benefits.

- **Thorough Testing**: Test asynchronous operations meticulously to ensure they handle load efficiently and behave predictably in high-concurrency environments.

Conclusion

Asynchronous database operations are essential for developing responsive, efficient, and scalable applications using ASP.NET Core and EF Core. By adopting asynchronous techniques, developers can ensure better resource management and more responsive applications, suitable for modern enterprise demands. These operations not only facilitate improved performance but also enhance user experiences by maintaining a fluid interaction with the application regardless of backend processes.

Chapter Nine

Authentication and Authorization

Security fundamentals

In today's tech-driven world, security stands as a critical pillar in software development, essential for establishing trust and ensuring robust system performance. Grasping the core principles of security is crucial for developers aiming to protect data integrity, ensure system resilience, and maintain authorized user interactions within software systems. This discussion delves into pivotal security principles and methodologies necessary for crafting secure applications.

Key Security Principles

At the heart of application security are three fundamental principles, commonly known as the CIA triad:

1. **Confidentiality**: This principle ensures that sensitive information is only accessible to those who are authorized. Methods to uphold confidentiality include encryption, the use of SSL for secure communications, and stringent access controls to maintain data privacy.

2. **Integrity**: This ensures data remains accurate and untampered across its lifecycle. Techniques like cryptographic hashing and digital signatures help safeguard data integrity by deterring unauthorized alterations.

3. **Availability**: This focuses on making sure that data and services are always accessible for authorized users, especially during critical times. This involves protecting against threats such as DDoS attacks, which can incapacitate system availability.

Implementing Security in Software Engineering

Building in security across the software development lifecycle involves multiple facets:

Secure Coding Practices

Incorporating secure coding practices is fundamental to shielding applications against potential vulnerabilities. Key practices include:

- **Input Validation**: Thoroughly validating all input data to prevent common vulnerabilities such as SQL injection, XSS, and command injection. Using parameterized queries or prepared statements is a direct way to mitigate these risks:

```
// Example of a parameterized query
SELECT * FROM users WHERE email = ?;
```

- **Authentication and Authorization**: Ensuring robust mechanisms are in place for verifying user identity and granting appropriate access based on user roles.

- **Error Management**: Carefully handling errors to prevent leakage of sensitive information or system details, and ensuring errors are logged accurately for auditing.

Encryption Techniques

Protecting data through encryption is critical both at rest and in transit:

- **Data at Rest**: Implementing strong encryption standards such as AES to encrypt stored data.

- **Data in Transit**: Using protocols like TLS to secure data being transmitted. Implementing HTTPS over HTTP is a standard practice to secure web interactions.

Strengthening Network Security

Enhancing network security involves configuring:

- **Firewalls and Routers**: These should be configured to control traffic based on pre-defined security rules.

- **VPNs**: Virtual Private Networks are crucial for securing remote network access.

- **Intrusion Detection Systems (IDS)**: Deploying IDS to monitor and respond to suspicious network activity.

Regular Security Reviews

Maintaining security requires continuous evaluation:

- Conduct regular security audits to identify and rectify vulnerabilities.

- Use code analysis tools to detect and fix security flaws effectively.

Compliance with Security Standards

Adhering to recognized security standards and regulations is essential, particularly for handling sensitive or personal data:

- **ISO/IEC 27001**: This international standard provides specifications for an information security management system (ISMS).

- **General Data Protection Regulation (GDPR)**: A framework for data protection and privacy in the European Union.

- **Payment Card Industry Data Security Standard (PCI DSS)**: A set of security standards designed to ensure all companies that accept, process, store, or transmit credit card information maintain a secure environment.

Conclusion

Security is not merely about deploying the right tools or following best practices; it's about fostering a security-centric culture throughout all phases of software development and operations. By embracing these foundational security principles and practices, developers can effectively shield their applications from existing and emerging threats, ensuring a secure and reliable digital environment.

Setting up authentication

Implementing strong authentication measures is crucial in safeguarding applications, ensuring controlled access to sensitive data and functionalities. Effective authentication protocols are vital in maintaining data privacy, confirming user identities, and preventing unauthorized access. This discussion will outline various robust strategies and technologies pivotal for integrating comprehensive authentication across diverse platforms.

Principles of Authentication

Authentication serves as the primary security gateway in digital applications, determining whether users or systems have authorization to access specified resources. It typically involves:

- **Knowledge factors**: Something the user knows (e.g., passwords, security questions).

- **Possession factors**: Something the user possesses (e.g., security tokens, mobile devices).

- **Inherence factors**: Something inherent to the user (e.g., biometric data like fingerprints or retinal scans).

Steps to Establish an Authentication System

Developing a dependable authentication system involves several critical steps, from selecting the appropriate authentication model to securely handling user credentials and designing interfaces for user interaction. Below are essential steps and considerations:

1. Selecting an Authentication Method

Choosing the correct authentication method should align with the application's security requirements and architecture:

- **Basic Authentication**: Simple but potentially less secure, involving sending usernames and passwords with each request.

- **Token-Based Authentication**: Utilizes security tokens, such as JWTs, that are issued at login and used for subsequent verification, enhancing performance and security.

- **OAuth**: Allows authentication through trusted third-party providers (e.g., Google, Facebook), bolstering security with external verification.

- **Multi-Factor Authentication (MFA)**: Enhances security by requiring multiple forms of verification before granting access.

2. Secure Management of Credentials

It's crucial to handle user credentials with high security:

- **Encryption**: Ensure all sensitive communication is encrypted using HTTPS.

- **Hashing**: Use strong cryptographic hashing algorithms, like bcrypt, to securely store passwords, incorporating salts to fend off attack strategies.

- **Password Policies**: Implement stringent password policies to prevent the reuse of passwords and promote the use of strong, complex passwords.

3. Creating Secure Registration and Login Modules

Develop secure modules for user registration and login:

- **Input Validation**: Perform thorough validation on the client and server sides to shield against common security threats like SQL Injection.

- **Rate Limiting**: Place limits on login attempts to defend against brute force attacks.

- **Error Handling**: Use generalized error messages that do not reveal specific details about authentication failures (e.g., "Invalid login credentials").

Example: Login System with ASP.NET Core

Here's how you might set up a basic login system in ASP.NET Core, utilizing the Identity framework for handling user authentication:

```csharp
public class AccountController : Controller
{
    private readonly SignInManager<ApplicationUser> _signInManager;

    public AccountController(SignInManager<ApplicationUser> signInManager)
    {
        _signInManager = signInManager;
    }

    [HttpPost]
    public async Task<IActionResult> Login(string username, string password)
    {
        // Try to authenticate the user
        var result = await _signInManager.PasswordSignInAsync(username,
            password, isPersistent: false, lockoutOnFailure: false);

        if (result.Succeeded)
        {
            return RedirectToAction("Index", "Home");
        }
        else
        {
            ModelState.AddModelError("", "Failed login attempt.");
            return View();
        }
    }
}
```

This snippet shows the usage of **SignInManager** for validating user credentials through the **PasswordSignInAsync** method.

Best Practices for Effective Authentication

- **Continuous Updates**: Regularly update and patch authentication-related systems to protect against emerging threats.

- **User Education**: Instruct users on creating strong passwords and recognizing phishing attempts.

- **Session Security**: Implement secure session management practices, including timely session expiration and secure storage of session identifiers.

Conclusion

Establishing robust authentication is essential for securing applications against unauthorized access and safeguarding user data. By deploying advanced authentication techniques and following established best practices, developers can significantly enhance the security infrastructure of their applications, ensuring a safe and reliable user experience.

Implementing authorization policies

Establishing strong authorization policies is critical for ensuring that users have the appropriate access to a system's resources. Authorization, which follows authentication, determines a user's permissions and what resources they can access within a system. Implementing effective authorization measures is essential to limit access to sensitive operations and data, thereby safeguarding system integrity and security. This article outlines effective practices for setting up authorization policies, with a focus on role-based access control (RBAC), attribute-based access control (ABAC), and policy-based access control systems.

Fundamentals of Authorization

Authorization acts as a key security mechanism by defining user privileges and access levels to system resources such as files, databases, and applications. This ensures users only access resources pertinent to their roles within an organization or system.

Key Strategies for Implementing Authorization Policies

1. Develop Clear Access Control Policies

The foundation of robust authorization is clear, comprehensive access control policies that outline permissions and conditions for access. These should be developed in collaboration with stakeholders from IT, security, and business operations to align with both security needs and business goals.

2. Implement Role-Based Access Control (RBAC)

RBAC simplifies the management of user permissions by associating roles with specific permissions and then assigning these roles to users based on their responsibilities.

- **Example of RBAC in ASP.NET Core:**

```csharp
public class Startup
{
    public void ConfigureServices(IServiceCollection services)
    {
        services.AddAuthorization(options =>
        {
            options.AddPolicy("RequireAdministratorRole",
                policy => policy.RequireRole("Administrator"));
        });
    }
}

[Authorize(Policy = "RequireAdministratorRole")]
public IActionResult AdminOnlyAction()
{
    // Code for action accessible only to administrators
    return View();
}
```

This example sets up an authorization policy in ASP.NET Core that restricts certain actions to users who have been assigned the "Administrator" role.

3. Use Attribute-Based Access Control (ABAC)

ABAC allows for flexibility by considering various attributes (user, system, environmental) in access decisions, offering granular control over who can access what under specific conditions.

- **ABAC Usage Scenario:**

In a corporate environment, an employee can access certain documents only if they are within the corporate network and during specified working hours.

4. Adopt Policy-Based Access Control

This approach leverages a central policy hub to manage access across different systems, enabling dynamic access control based on evolving conditions.

- **Example Using Policy Decision Point (PDP):**

```
if (user.role == "Executive" and (document.classification == "secret" and access
    .location == "HQ"))
    grant access
else
    deny access
```

This example illustrates a policy where access is granted based on multiple contextual factors, ensuring decisions are made dynamically.

5. Regularly Audit and Update Access Controls

As roles evolve and business needs change, it's crucial to regularly review and update access controls to ensure they remain effective and relevant.

6. Educate and Train Stakeholders

Educating users and administrators about access control policies and practices enhances compliance and security posture.

Embedding Authorization in Software Development

During development, integrate authorization checks directly into the application's business logic, utilizing built-in support from development frameworks to enforce security policies effectively.

Conclusion

Properly implemented authorization policies are vital for maintaining secure and efficient access to a system's resources. By using methodologies like RBAC, ABAC, and dynamic policy-based controls, and ensuring regular updates and education, organizations can protect sensitive data and systems from unauthorized access while supporting operational efficiency. Effective authorization is a cornerstone of a holistic security strategy.

Protecting API endpoints

In today's digital landscape, APIs (Application Programming Interfaces) are essential for enabling the seamless interactions between different software platforms. Given their critical role in data exchange and system functionality, protecting API endpoints from security threats is vital to prevent unauthorized access and ensure the continuity of services. This article explores a range of strategies for enhancing the security of API endpoints, highlighting essential practices in the context of contemporary software development.

Essentials of API Security

APIs facilitate the integration of various systems, exposing them to potential cyber threats such as data breaches, denial of service (DoS) attacks, and man-in-the-middle attacks. Implementing rigorous security measures to defend these endpoints is crucial for protecting the data and functionalities they expose.

Key Approaches to Securing API Endpoints

1. Mandate HTTPS for All Data Transmissions

Encrypting data transmitted between clients and servers using HTTPS is fundamental. HTTPS utilizes TLS (Transport Layer Security) to ensure that data is securely encrypted, thereby safeguarding its confidentiality and integrity during transit.

- **Implementation Advice**: Configure all servers to redirect HTTP traffic to HTTPS and implement HTTP Strict Transport Security (HSTS) to strengthen enforcement.

2. Employ Robust Authentication and Authorization

Verifying user identities and controlling access to APIs is crucial. Implement reliable authentication mechanisms such as OAuth2, OpenID Connect, or API keys to manage user identities and their access privileges accurately.

- **.NET Example for Authorization with JWT**:

```
[Authorize]
public class SecureApiController : ControllerBase
{
    public IActionResult AccessSecureData()
    {
        // This method is secured to ensure only authenticated users can access it
        return Ok("Secure data accessed successfully.");
    }
}
```

This example in ASP.NET Core uses JWTs to authenticate users, with the **[Authorize]** attribute restricting access to the method to authenticated users only.

3. Thoroughly Validate and Sanitize Inputs

To guard against vulnerabilities such as SQL injection and XSS, it is essential to validate and sanitize all API inputs thoroughly. This ensures they adhere to the expected formats and are free from malicious content.

- **Security Practice**: Use rigorous validation techniques and adopt libraries that help in sanitizing inputs to protect against various security threats.

4. Implement Rate Limiting

Rate limiting is an effective control to prevent API abuse and protect against DoS attacks. By limiting the number of requests that can be made in a given period, you can help protect the API from being overwhelmed.

- **Implementation in Express.js**:

```
const rateLimit = require("express-rate-limit");
const apiLimiter = rateLimit({
    windowMs: 15 * 60 * 1000, // 15 minutes
    max: 100 // limits each IP to 100 requests per window
});

// Apply this rate limiting to all API endpoints
app.use(apiLimiter);
```

5. Utilize API Gateways

API gateways provide a robust framework for managing API traffic. They handle routing, load balancing, and enforce security policies such as authentication and rate limiting.

6. Monitor and Log All API Traffic

Effective monitoring and logging are vital for identifying and responding to security incidents quickly. Ensure comprehensive logging of API usage to facilitate the detection of any abnormal activities or security breaches.

- **Logging Strategy**: Develop an advanced logging infrastructure that meticulously records detailed user interactions and security incidents for analysis.

7. Regularly Update APIs and Dependencies

Continuously updating API frameworks and libraries is essential to address known vulnerabilities and enhance security features, thus keeping the APIs secure against new threats.

Conclusion

Securing API endpoints is crucial for the safe operation of software systems in the interconnected world of today. By enforcing HTTPS, implementing strong authentication, performing input validation, applying rate limiting, leveraging API gateways, and maintaining vigilant monitoring and updates, organizations can significantly fortify their API security frameworks. As APIs increasingly become integral to technological ecosystems, prioritizing their security is fundamental to safeguarding critical data and ensuring operational integrity.

Chapter Ten

Testing Web APIs

Types of tests: unit, integration

In software engineering, testing forms a critical phase that ensures the application behaves as intended and minimizes potential defects. Two fundamental types of testing, unit testing and integration testing, are integral to a successful testing strategy. Each type addresses different aspects of the software, using distinct methodologies to improve software reliability and robustness.

Unit Testing

Unit testing targets the smallest testable parts of an application, typically individual functions or methods, to ensure they operate correctly. This type of testing focuses on isolated examination of each component without interaction with other parts of the system.

Goals of Unit Testing:

- **Functional Assurance**: Validates that each function or component performs as designed.

- **Early Bug Detection**: Helps in identifying and resolving bugs during the development phase, thus reducing future remediation costs.

- **Support for Refactoring**: Allows developers to refactor code with confidence, as any breakages in functionality will be quickly highlighted by failing tests.

Characteristics of Unit Testing:

- **Isolation**: Tests are run in isolation, without reliance on external systems or interactions.

- **Automatability**: Unit tests are typically automated, enabling them to be run quickly and as often as needed without additional expense.

- **Repeatability**: Tests are designed to produce the same outcomes under consistent conditions across multiple runs.

Example of Unit Testing in Python:

Consider testing a simple function, **add**, which sums two numbers. Here's how you might test this function using Python's **unittest** module:

```python
import unittest

def add(a, b):
    return a + b

class TestAddFunction(unittest.TestCase):
    def test_add(self):
        self.assertEqual(add(1, 2), 3)
        self.assertEqual(add(-1, 1), 0)
        self.assertEqual(add(-1, -1), -2)

if __name__ == '__main__':
    unittest.main()
```

This test suite, **TestAddFunction**, verifies that the **add** function accurately calculates the sums of various pairs of integers.

Integration Testing

Integration testing assesses the collective operation of multiple units or modules to identify defects in their interactions. This testing phase is critical for catching issues that might not be visible during unit testing, such as problems with data formats or interfaces between components.

Objectives of Integration Testing:

- **Interface Defect Detection**: Focuses on identifying problems in the interaction between integrated units.

- **Comprehensive System Evaluation**: Verifies that the entire system functions correctly and meets specified requirements when components are combined.

- **Performance Verification**: Tests the system's performance under integrated scenarios to ensure it meets predefined benchmarks.

Features of Integration Testing:

- **Incremental Methodology**: Often conducted incrementally by integrating and testing components step by step or adding them to a previously tested group.

- **Scenario-Based Testing**: Involves testing based on scenarios that are likely to occur during normal system usage.

Example of Integration Testing in Python:

Expanding on the previous unit test, imagine integrating the **add** function with another function that calculates averages:

```python
def average(numbers):
    return add(sum(numbers), len(numbers))

class TestIntegration(unittest.TestCase):
    def test_average_integration(self):
        self.assertEqual(average([1, 2, 3, 4]), 2.5)
        self.assertEqual(average([1, -1]), 0)
        self.assertEqual(average([-1, -1, -1]), -1)

if __name__ == '__main__':
    unittest.main()
```

Here, the **TestIntegration** class checks how the **add** and **average** functions perform together, ensuring they integrate seamlessly.

Conclusion

Both unit and integration testing are crucial for developing stable and dependable software. Unit tests scrutinize individual components for correct behavior, while integration tests ensure that these components interact properly. Together, these testing types enhance the quality and reliability of software, streamline maintenance, and support agile methodologies by allowing developers to make changes with assurance, ultimately leading to a more robust final product.

Testing frameworks for ASP.NET Core

Testing is a critical component of software development that confirms whether an application meets its specifications and functions correctly. In the ASP.NET Core environment, several testing frameworks are available to help developers ensure their applications are robust and error-free. This article explores notable testing frameworks suited for ASP.NET Core, discussing their features, advantages, and providing examples of their use.

xUnit.net

xUnit.net is a popular choice within the .NET community for testing, especially favored for its modern structure and flexibility in handling various testing scenarios for ASP.NET Core applications.

Features:

- **Extensibility and Flexibility**: Allows for customization of test patterns and assertions, making it highly adaptable for complex testing needs.

- **Parameterized Tests**: Supports extensive data-driven testing with features like inline data, class data, and member data.

- **Parallel Execution**: Capable of running tests in parallel, which can reduce the time it takes to execute extensive test suites.

Example Usage:

Here's an example demonstrating how to use xUnit.net for testing multiple inputs using inline data:

```csharp
public class CalculatorTests
{
    [Theory]
    [InlineData(5, 2, 7)]
    [InlineData(-1, -1, -2)]
    [InlineData(-1, 1, 0)]
    public void Add_Values_ReturnsCorrectSum(int value1, int value2, int expectedSum)
    {
        var calculator = new Calculator();
        var result = calculator.Add(value1, value2);
        Assert.Equal(expectedSum, result);
    }
}
```

```csharp
public class Calculator
{
    public int Add(int x, int y)
    {
        return x + y;
    }
}
```

This test class, **CalculatorTests**, demonstrates the **Add** function's correctness across several different cases using the **Theory** and **InlineData** attributes.

NUnit

NUnit is another robust framework used extensively for .NET applications. It's known for its rich feature set and flexibility in handling different types of tests, from simple unit tests to complex integration tests.

Features:

- **Parametric Testing**: Excellent support for writing complex tests with varied inputs.

- **Setup and Teardown**: Offers detailed options for initializing and cleaning up test contexts.

- **Integration with Tools**: Seamlessly works with various tools and CI systems, enhancing its utility in professional development environments.

Example Usage:

Here's how you might set up tests in NUnit to handle multiple scenarios with different inputs:

```csharp
[TestFixture]
public class CalculatorTests
{
    private Calculator _calculator;

    [SetUp]
    public void Initialize()
    {
        _calculator = new Calculator();
    }
```

```csharp
[Test]
[TestCase(5, 2, 7)]
[TestCase(-1, -1, -2)]
[TestCase(-1, 1, 0)]
public void Add_Values_ReturnsCorrectSum(int value1, int value2, int expectedSum)
{
    var result = _calculator.Add(value1, value2);
    Assert.That(result, Is.EqualTo(expectedSum));
}
}
```

The **TestCase** attribute is used here to provide different data sets directly in the test methods, simplifying data-driven testing.

MSTest

MSTest is the testing framework developed by Microsoft, heavily integrated into the Visual Studio environment. It is particularly preferred by teams looking for a tight integration with their development environment.

Features:

- **Deep Visual Studio Integration**: Offers built-in test runners and explorers for a seamless user experience.

- **Data-Driven Testing**: Robust support for data-driven tests, pulling data from various sources.

- **Code Coverage**: Integrates smoothly with Visual Studio's code coverage tools, helping developers understand which parts of the codebase are being tested.

Example Usage:

Here's a simple MSTest example demonstrating data-driven tests:

```
[TestClass]
public class CalculatorTests
{
    [TestMethod]
    [DataRow(5, 2, 7)]
    [DataRow(-1, -1, -2)]
    [DataRow(-1, 1, 0)]
    public void Add_Values_ReturnsCorrectSum(int value1, int value2, int expectedSum)
```

```
{
    var calculator = new Calculator();
    var result = calculator.Add(value1, value2);
    Assert.AreEqual(expectedSum, result);
}
}
```

This example uses the **DataRow** attribute to feed multiple sets of values into the test method, facilitating straightforward data-driven tests.

Conclusion

Selecting the right testing framework for ASP.NET Core often depends on the project requirements, team preferences, and the specific features needed for testing. xUnit.net, NUnit, and MSTest each offer distinct advantages that can help ensure high-quality applications. By integrating these frameworks into their development processes, developers can achieve comprehensive test coverage and maintain high standards of software quality.

Writing testable code

Creating testable code is a critical aspect of software development, enhancing the robustness, maintainability, and operational integrity of applications. Such code facilitates easier validation through automated tests, ensuring the application functions as anticipated and minimizes bug occurrences. This article presents strategies for developing testable code, emphasizing the principles, design patterns, and practices that enhance both software quality and testability.

Core Principles for Testable Code

1. **Single Responsibility Principle (SRP)**: This principle suggests that each module or class should only have one reason to change, focusing on a single functionality. This specialization makes the module or class easier to test and maintain.

2. **Dependency Injection (DI)**: Dependency Injection is a technique related to the broader Inversion of Control (IoC) principle that improves a system's modularity and testability. By supplying an object's dependencies from outside rather than hard-coding them within the object, it becomes easier to manage and test those dependencies, typically using mocks or stubs in tests.

3. **Interface Segregation Principle (ISP)**: By promoting the use of multiple, specific interfaces rather than a single, general-purpose interface, this principle helps reduce the complexity of implementations, making them easier to test and maintain.

4. **Prefer Composition Over Inheritance**: Favoring composition over inheritance can avoid issues associated with deep inheritance chains and tight coupling, which often complicate testing and maintenance.

Practices to Enhance Testability

1. **Eliminate Global State and Side Effects**: Code that relies on global states or produces side effects can be unpredictable and difficult to test. Striving for pure

functions, where the output is solely determined by the input and there are no external interactions, can simplify testing.

2. **Leverage Mocks and Stubs**: Replace external dependencies like databases or web services with mocks or stubs during unit testing to isolate the code under test and ensure the tests are both faster and more reliable.

3. **Adopt Test-Driven Development (TDD)**: Writing tests before developing the corresponding functionalities can guide software design towards simplicity and high test coverage, inherently leading to more testable code.

4. **Utilize Parameterized Testing**: Designing tests that accept parameters can help streamline and extend test suites more efficiently, enhancing both test coverage and maintainability.

5. **Maintain Clean and Readable Test Code**: Ensuring that test code is as well-cared-for as production code, with clear naming and structured formatting, helps maintain the effectiveness and maintainability of tests.

Example in C# Using ASP.NET Core

Consider implementing a service in an ASP.NET Core application that interacts with a database. By abstracting the database interactions behind an interface and injecting this interface, you can enhance testability as shown below:

```csharp
public interface IDataRepository
{
    Task<Item> GetItemAsync(int id);
}
```

```csharp
public class MyService
{
    private readonly IDataRepository _repository;

    public MyService(IDataRepository repository)
    {
        _repository = repository;
    }

    public async Task<Item> GetItem(int id)
    {
        return await _repository.GetItemAsync(id);
    }
}

public class MyServiceTests
{
    [Fact]
    public async Task GetItem_ReturnsExpectedItem()
    {
        // Arrange
        var mockRepository = new Mock<IDataRepository>();
        mockRepository.Setup(repo => repo.GetItemAsync(1)).ReturnsAsync(new
            Item { Id = 1, Name = "TestItem" });
        var service = new MyService(mockRepository.Object);
```

```csharp
        // Act
        var result = await service.GetItem(1);

        // Assert
        Assert.NotNull(result);
        Assert.Equal("TestItem", result.Name);
    }
}
```

This code segment demonstrates how **MyService** relies on **IDataRepository**, a dependency that is injected and can be easily mocked in tests. This setup allows for precise control during testing and simplifies verifying behavior under various conditions.

Conclusion

Writing testable code requires thoughtful design and disciplined practice. It's not just a technique but a fundamental approach that influences the entire development lifecycle. By adhering to principles such as SRP and DI, and employing practices like TDD and the use of mocks, developers can create software that is easier to maintain, more robust, and highly reliable. These practices do not merely facilitate testing—they enhance the overall architecture and longevity of the software.

Mocking dependencies

In the landscape of software development, especially within unit testing, the practice of mocking dependencies is vital for isolating specific sections of code to ensure they are tested in a clean environment. Mocking involves substituting real operational dependencies with mock objects that mimic the behavior of these dependencies. This method is particularly valuable when dealing with components that are complex, slow, or unavailable, enabling controlled and repeatable tests.

The Role of Mocking

Mocking serves to simulate the behavior of external dependencies in a controlled manner, allowing developers to verify the interactions and functionalities of different parts of an application independently from external systems or databases.

Advantages of Mocking Dependencies

1. **Isolation**: Mocks create an isolated testing environment for each unit of code, preventing failures in one area from cascading to others and helping identify the exact points of failure.

2. **Simplification**: Replacing a complex dependency with a mock simplifies the testing process by removing the intricacies and variability associated with the actual dependency.

3. **Control**: With mocking, developers can precisely dictate the responses from dependencies, ranging from successful outputs to throwing exceptions, thus testing various scenarios and edge cases.

4. **Efficiency**: Tests involving mocks run significantly faster than those accessing real databases or networks, speeding up the development cycle.

5. **Accessibility**: Mocks can stand in for dependencies that are costly, difficult to set up, or not yet available during the initial phases of development.

Methods for Implementing Mocks

Mocking can be realized through different methods, tailored to suit specific testing needs:

1. **Mocking Frameworks**: Tools such as Moq, NSubstitute, or Rhino Mocks in .NET are designed to facilitate the creation of dynamic mocks that can simulate almost any behavior of dependencies without manually coding the mock objects.

2. **Manual Mocks**: In simpler scenarios, developers might opt to manually write their mock objects. This approach provides direct control but may become inefficient as the required behavior grows in complexity.

3. **Fakes and Stubs**: These are less complex alternatives to full-fledged mocks, suitable when the test only needs to simulate part of the functionality of the real dependencies.

Mocking Best Practices

1. **Appropriate Use of Mocks**: While powerful, mocks should be used when genuinely beneficial, avoiding over-mocking which can lead to brittle tests that do not represent real-world scenarios.

2. **Maintain Simplicity in Mocks**: Mocks should be kept as straightforward as possible, mimicking only the necessary behaviors required for the tests to avoid introducing unnecessary complexity into the test suite.

3. **Interaction Verification**: Many mocking frameworks offer capabilities to verify interactions with the mocks, such as checking that certain methods were called with expected parameters, which is crucial for ensuring correct system behavior.

C# Example Using Moq

Consider the following example where Moq is used to mock a data service in an ASP.NET Core application:

```csharp
public interface IDataService
{
    Task<string> GetDataAsync();
}
```

```csharp
public class MyService
{
    private readonly IDataService _dataService;

    public MyService(IDataService dataService)
    {
        _dataService = dataService;
    }

    public async Task<string> ProcessDataAsync()
    {
        var data = await _dataService.GetDataAsync();
        return data.ToUpper(); // Example processing
    }
}
```

```csharp
public class MyServiceTests
{
    [Fact]
    public async Task ProcessDataAsync_ReturnsUpperCasedData()
    {
        // Arrange
        var mockDataService = new Mock<IDataService>();
        mockDataService.Setup(service => service.GetDataAsync()).ReturnsAsync("test data");

        var service = new MyService(mockDataService.Object);

        // Act
        var result = await service.ProcessDataAsync();

        // Assert
        Assert.Equal("TEST DATA", result);
    }
}
```

This snippet demonstrates how **IDataService** is mocked to control the output of the **GetDataAsync** method, allowing the test to focus exclusively on verifying the behavior of **MyService.ProcessDataAsync**.

Conclusion

Mastering the technique of mocking is essential for developers aiming to enhance the reliability and maintainability of their software through effective unit testing. By strategically using mocks to simulate complex systems and interactions, developers can ensure their tests are both comprehensive and efficient, ultimately leading to higher quality and more robust software solutions.

Chapter Eleven

API Versioning and Documentation

Why versioning is important

Versioning in software development is a critical process where different versions of software are marked with unique identifiers throughout its development cycle. This systematic approach is crucial for effectively managing software changes and ensuring application stability as it matures. Adopting robust versioning practices can greatly enhance software deployment and maintenance, providing key advantages in managing developmental complexities, boosting user engagement, and facilitating smooth release and dependency management processes.

Importance of Versioning

1. **Documentation and Progress Tracking**: Versioning serves as a detailed record of the software's evolution, documenting all changes, features, and fixes over time. This historical insight is invaluable for tracing the development process, pinpointing when specific changes were implemented, and identifying the contributors involved.

2. **Enhanced Team Collaboration**: Versioning is vital in multi-developer environments as it helps coordinate the contributions from multiple team members. It

ensures that individual modifications are merged seamlessly, preventing data overlaps or conflicts.

3. **Streamlined Release Management**: Versioning delineates the various stages of software development, such as testing, staging, and production, by tagging each release with a unique identifier. This clarity is crucial for managing deployment processes systematically.

4. **Effective Dependency Management**: In cases where software relies on third-party libraries or frameworks, versioning is essential to maintain compatibility. It helps manage dependencies carefully to avoid conflicts from incompatible updates.

5. **Safe Reversibility**: Versioning allows developers to revert the software to a previous state if new updates introduce bugs or fail. This capability is critical for maintaining stability and ensuring continuity of service.

6. **Improved User Experience**: Clear versioning informs users about new updates, bug fixes, and features, helping them decide when to update their software. It also aids support teams in troubleshooting by identifying the versions that are causing issues.

Strategies for Versioning

Semantic Versioning (SemVer) is a popular method due to its structured approach. It employs a versioning format of **MAJOR.MINOR.PATCH**:

- **MAJOR version** changes indicate significant updates that may break backward compatibility,

- **MINOR version** changes introduce new features that are backward-compatible,

- **PATCH version** includes fixes for backward-compatible issues.

This structured approach ensures that each version increment is meaningful and reflects the extent of changes introduced.

Practical Application of Semantic Versioning

For instance, a software project might utilize Semantic Versioning in the following manner:

```
Initial release: 1.0.0
Post-minor feature additions: 1.1.0
Following major changes affecting compatibility: 2.0.0
After a critical bug fix: 2.0.1
```

This versioning clearly communicates the nature and impact of changes to developers, operational staff, and users, aiding in better management and adaptation.

Versioning Challenges

Despite its benefits, versioning can present challenges such as over-versioning, where too frequent updates may overwhelm users, and under-versioning, where infrequent updates can lead to significant shifts in functionality that are hard for users to manage. Both scenarios can introduce broader bugs due to the scale of changes involved.

Conclusion

Versioning is fundamental to software development, playing a crucial role in managing changes, facilitating team collaboration, and organizing software releases. It ensures robust dependency management and enhances user experiences by providing transparency regarding software developments. As projects grow in complexity, a deliberate and strategic approach to versioning becomes increasingly important, underscoring the need for meticulous planning and execution of versioning practices to support effective software development and ensure the delivery of high-quality software products.

Implementing versioning in ASP.NET Core

Incorporating versioning into ASP.NET Core applications is an essential practice for managing the evolution of APIs and ensuring that updates do not disrupt existing users. Versioning enables backward compatibility, enhances communication with stakeholders about changes, and facilitates the maintenance of different API versions concurrently. ASP.NET Core offers robust mechanisms for implementing versioning, which allows developers to adopt a structured approach to manage changes effectively.

The Role of Versioning in ASP.NET Core

Versioning in ASP.NET Core is critical for several reasons:

1. **Backward Compatibility**: Versioning preserves functionality for existing clients even as new features are introduced or existing features are modified or phased out.

2. **Transparency with Changes**: Versioning clarifies the modifications between API versions, helping clients understand the implications of updates.

3. **Parallel Maintenance**: It allows different versions of an API to be maintained simultaneously, giving users the flexibility to upgrade at their convenience.

Common Versioning Strategies

ASP.NET Core supports multiple versioning strategies, each suitable for different scenarios:

1. **URI Versioning**: This involves including the version number directly in the API's URI path. It's straightforward and easily understandable.

2. **Query String Versioning**: Here, the version number is specified as a query parameter in the URL. This method maintains a clean URI structure.

3. **Header Versioning**: Version information is carried in the HTTP request headers, keeping the URL unchanged and clean.

4. **Media Type Versioning**: Also known as content negotiation or accept header versioning, where the version information is included in the media type of the request.

Implementing URI Versioning in ASP.NET Core

URI versioning is a popular method due to its simplicity and clarity. Here's how to implement it in an ASP.NET Core application:

1. **Install Necessary Packages**: Begin by installing the Microsoft.AspNetCore.Mvc.Versioning package via NuGet.

2. **Configure the Service**: Add and set up API versioning in the **ConfigureServices** method in Startup.cs.

```
public void ConfigureServices(IServiceCollection services)
{
    services.AddApiVersioning(options =>
    {
        options.DefaultApiVersion = new ApiVersion(1, 0); // Default to version 1.0
        options.AssumeDefaultVersionWhenUnspecified = true;
        options.ReportApiVersions = true;
        options.ApiVersionReader = new UrlSegmentApiVersionReader(); // Versioning through URL segment
    });
}
```

3. **Apply Versioning in Controllers**: Define the versions a controller supports using the **[ApiVersion]** attribute and configure the routing accordingly.

```
[ApiController]
[Route("api/v{version:apiVersion}/[controller]")]
public class ProductsController : ControllerBase
{
    [HttpGet]
    public IActionResult Get() => Ok("Version 1.0");

    [HttpGet, MapToApiVersion("2.0")]
    public IActionResult GetV2() => Ok("Version 2.0");
}
```

In this configuration, **ProductsController** supports multiple versions. The base endpoint returns "Version 1.0", and there is a specific action that will return "Version 2.0" when accessed with the version number in the URL.

Best Practices for Effective Versioning

- **Integrate Early**: Embed versioning early in the development process to ensure the API is designed with future changes in mind.

- **Graceful Deprecation**: Provide clear deprecation notices and continue supporting older API versions for a reasonable period to allow users to transition smoothly.

- **Adopt Semantic Versioning**: Utilize Semantic Versioning (SemVer) to indicate the nature of changes (major, minor, patch) clearly and help users gauge the impact of upgrading.

- **Maintain Comprehensive Documentation**: Keep detailed documentation of API changes per version to assist developers in integrating with or migrating to newer versions.

Conclusion

Implementing versioning in ASP.NET Core not only supports a sustainable development lifecycle but also enhances the manageability of APIs. By choosing a suitable versioning strategy and adhering to established best practices, developers can ensure that their APIs remain functional, reliable, and user-friendly across various updates, fostering a stable and progressive development environment.

Using Swagger for API documentation

In contemporary software development, especially for web APIs, clear and effective documentation is critical. It enhances the developer experience, facilitates smoother integrations, and accelerates the onboarding process. Swagger, also known as OpenAPI, is a key tool in this realm, offering a robust framework for documenting RESTful web services. This open-source platform assists developers in defining, building, and engaging with web services through a detailed, language-independent interface.

Introduction to Swagger (OpenAPI)

Swagger provides a universal interface for REST APIs, making them accessible and understandable without requiring direct access to the source code. It details the structure of APIs, including parameters, possible responses, and error handling, which aids significantly in both the design and testing stages of development.

Implementing Swagger in ASP.NET Core

Integrating Swagger into an ASP.NET Core application via Swashbuckle.AspNetCore enhances its capabilities for creating interactive and comprehensive API documentation. Here's how to integrate Swagger effectively:

1. **Installation**: Begin by installing the Swashbuckle.AspNetCore package via NuGet:

```
Install-Package Swashbuckle.AspNetCore
```

2. **Configuration in Startup.cs**: Incorporate Swagger in your project's **Startup.cs** file by configuring the Swagger generator and enabling middleware to serve the Swagger UI and JSON.

```
public class Startup
{
    public void ConfigureServices(IServiceCollection services)
    {
        services.AddSwaggerGen(c =>
        {
            c.SwaggerDoc("v1", new OpenApiInfo { Title = "My API", Version = "v1" });
        });
    }

    public void Configure(IApplicationBuilder app, IWebHostEnvironment env)
    {
        // Middleware to serve Swagger JSON
        app.UseSwagger();

        // Middleware to serve the Swagger UI
        app.UseSwaggerUI(c =>
        {
            c.SwaggerEndpoint("/swagger/v1/swagger.json", "My API V1");
            c.RoutePrefix = string.Empty; // Serve the Swagger UI at the root of
                the app
        });
    }
}
```

3. **Usage**: After setup, the root URL of your application will display the Swagger UI. This interface is not just informative but interactive, allowing users to directly execute API calls from the browser.

Benefits of Using Swagger

Swagger offers multiple advantages that make it indispensable for modern API development:

- **Interactive Documentation**: Swagger produces not only readable but also interactive documentation, which developers can use to execute API requests directly from their browsers, greatly simplifying testing and troubleshooting.

- **Automated Client SDK Generation**: Swagger can automatically generate client-side SDKs in various programming languages based on the API's specifications, streamlining client-side development.

- **Support for Design-First Approach**: By enabling API design and mock testing before coding, Swagger ensures thorough pre-development testing of API interfaces, promoting more robust design and implementation.

- **Widespread Tooling and Community Support**: Thanks to its popularity, Swagger is supported by a comprehensive ecosystem of tools and has a strong community, enhancing its functionality and integration capabilities.

Conclusion

Adopting Swagger within ASP.NET Core applications significantly boosts the effectiveness of API documentation and management. By leveraging Swagger, developers can not only enhance their workflow efficiencies but also improve communication and interaction with APIs. This structured approach to API management ensures better development practices and superior service interoperability, making APIs more robust, user-friendly, and comprehensible.

Customizing the Swagger UI

Refining the Swagger UI to suit the specific requirements of your web applications can greatly improve the developer experience by making API documentation more user-friendly and visually integrated with your brand identity. The Swagger UI is crucial not only for API documentation but also as the initial platform many developers interact with. Customizing it to align better with your organization's style and functional needs can result in a more engaging and productive user interaction.

Importance of Customizing Swagger UI

Adjusting the Swagger UI's aesthetic and functional elements to meet specific organizational requirements or user preferences can involve a variety of changes. These might include simple aesthetic tweaks such as updating the UI's color scheme or logo, to more extensive functional enhancements like adding custom functionalities or advanced security features.

Reasons to Customize Swagger UI

1. **Brand Alignment**: Tailoring the Swagger UI to match your company's branding helps strengthen your brand identity and ensures a uniform experience across all customer touchpoints.

2. **Enhanced Usability**: By improving the layout of the documentation, organizing API endpoints more effectively, enhancing descriptions, or incorporating usage examples, the Swagger UI becomes more intuitive and easier to navigate.

3. **Security Enhancements**: Incorporating security measures such as API key integration or OAuth authentication directly into the Swagger UI can secure API testing and interactions from the documentation interface.

4. **Personalized Functionality**: Adding specific features that cater to the needs of your API users, like support for custom headers or interactive examples, can significantly increase the utility and user-friendliness of your API documentation.

Customizing Swagger UI in ASP.NET Core with Swashbuckle.AspNetCore

Customizing the Swagger UI in an ASP.NET Core application facilitated by Swashbuckle.AspNetCore involves several straightforward steps:

1. **Swashbuckle Installation**: Begin by ensuring that Swashbuckle is installed in your project to enable full Swagger support within ASP.NET Core, done via NuGet:

```
Install-Package Swashbuckle.AspNetCore
```

2. **Configuration in Startup.cs**: Implement Swagger setup in your project's **Startup.cs** file to activate and serve the Swagger JSON and the customizable UI.

```csharp
public void ConfigureServices(IServiceCollection services)
{
    services.AddSwaggerGen(c =>
    {
        c.SwaggerDoc("v1", new OpenApiInfo { Title = "My API", Version = "v1" });
    });
}

public void Configure(IApplicationBuilder app, IWebHostEnvironment env)
{
    app.UseSwagger();
    app.UseSwaggerUI(c =>
    {
        c.SwaggerEndpoint("/swagger/v1/swagger.json", "My API V1");
    });
}
```

3. **UI Customization**: Modify the Swagger UI's appearance by introducing custom CSS or altering the HTML template.

      o **Custom CSS Implementation**: Adjust the visual style by specifying a custom CSS file within the Swagger UI options:

```csharp
app.UseSwaggerUI(c =>
{
    c.InjectStylesheet("/path/to/custom.css"); // Specify the custom CSS file location
});
```

- **Custom Index.html**: For comprehensive modifications, utilize a custom **index.html**:

```
app.UseSwaggerUI(c =>
{
    c.IndexStream = () => GetType().GetTypeInfo().Assembly
      .GetManifestResourceStream("YourAssemblyName.custom-index.html"); //
         Substitute 'YourAssemblyName' with your actual assembly name
});
```

4. **Add Custom Scripts**: Extend or refine the Swagger UI's functionality by integrating custom JavaScript.

    - **Custom JavaScript**: Enhance functionality by linking to a custom JavaScript file:

```
app.UseSwaggerUI(c =>
{
    c.InjectJavascript("/path/to/custom.js"); // Provide the path to your custom
        JavaScript file
});
```

Conclusion

Customizing the Swagger UI can turn a standard API documentation interface into a sophisticated, brand-cohesive developer portal. By improving both its visual appeal and functionality, you not only enhance its attractiveness but also its effectiveness and security. Proper customization ensures that your API is showcased optimally, fostering better engagement and aligning seamlessly with broader business objectives and technical strategies.

Chapter Twelve

Enhancing API Performance

Understanding performance issues

Grasping performance issues in software applications is crucial for ensuring they run efficiently and effectively. Such issues can significantly impact user satisfaction, operational costs, and the overall reliability of systems. Properly identifying, diagnosing, and resolving these issues are fundamental steps in maintaining any software system's integrity.

Defining Performance Issues

Performance problems in software systems generally relate to issues of speed, responsiveness, and resource utilization. These can manifest as delays in application response, slow data processing, excessive consumption of memory, or difficulties in scaling when user demand increases.

1. **Speed and Latency**: These are the most directly observable issues. Users might notice slow page loading times or operations that take longer than they should. High latency, where the system is slow to respond to user inputs, also falls into this category.

2. **Resource Utilization**: This involves the inefficient use of system resources such as CPU, memory, and disk space, which can lead to performance bottlenecks. Overuse can hinder not only the problematic

application but also other applications running on the same system.

3. **Concurrency and Scalability**: Issues here arise when an application cannot handle an increase in workload efficiently. This could be due to poor database management practices, ineffective caching strategies, or inadequate web server configuration.

Identifying Performance Issues

Detecting performance problems typically involves a combination of monitoring, testing, and profiling:

- **Monitoring**: Ongoing observation of applications and their hosting infrastructure helps in recognizing anomalies in performance. Real-time monitoring tools like New Relic, Dynatrace, and Prometheus offer valuable insights into application behavior and resource usage.

- **Profiling**: This technique analyzes how an application spends its time or consumes memory during execution. Profiling tools can help identify inefficient code paths, memory leaks, or redundant database queries.

- **Load Testing**: By simulating user interactions with the application, developers can observe how it performs under various load conditions. Tools such as JMeter, LoadRunner, or Apache Bench are commonly used for this purpose.

Diagnosing Performance Issues

After identifying performance anomalies, diagnosing them is critical to uncover their root causes. Common diagnostic strategies include:

- **Analyzing Logs**: Log files can reveal what the application was doing when performance dipped. Searching logs for errors, slow transactions, or resource alerts can provide clues.

- **Using APM Tools**: Application Performance Management (APM) tools deliver detailed insights into how different components of an application stack perform and interact, which is invaluable for troubleshooting.

- **Database Query Optimization**: Often, performance issues stem from inefficient database queries. Tools like SQL Profiler or the EXPLAIN command in SQL databases help understand and optimize query performance.

Example of Performance Diagnosis

Consider a scenario where a web application is experiencing slow response times. An investigation using an APM tool like MiniProfiler reveals that database queries are the bottleneck. Further analysis with a tool like SQL Profiler shows that the queries are not optimized. For instance:

```sql
-- Sample query without an index
SELECT * FROM Users WHERE LastName = 'Smith';
```

If the **Users** table is large, this query can be slow because it must scan each row. Adding an index on **LastName** could significantly improve performance:

```sql
-- Adding an index to improve query performance
CREATE INDEX idx_lastname ON Users(LastName);
```

Implementing this index would likely decrease the query's execution time, improving the application's responsiveness.

Mitigating Performance Issues

To effectively address performance issues, consider the following approaches:

- **Optimization**: Based on diagnostics, optimize code, queries, and system configurations. This may involve code refactoring, query optimization, or resource scaling.

- **Adherence to Best Practices**: Implement performance best practices, such as optimizing memory usage, choosing appropriate data structures, and minimizing computation within loops.

- **Regular Performance Audits**: Conducting periodic performance reviews can help catch and mitigate issues before they impact users.

Conclusion

Understanding and resolving performance issues is an essential, continuous challenge that necessitates a structured approach to monitor, diagnose, and mitigate problems effectively. Employing the right tools and practices allows developers to proactively manage performance issues, ensuring software applications remain robust and efficient while providing a positive user experience.

Caching strategies

Caching stands as a pivotal optimization tactic in software development, aimed at enhancing application performance by temporarily storing frequently accessed data or files. This approach reduces the need to continuously retrieve data from slower, primary storage or to recompute complex operations, leading to faster access times and a more efficient user experience. This discussion delves into various caching strategies, detailing their implementation and potential impacts on system efficiency.

Fundamentals of Caching

Caching involves storing copies of frequently accessed data in a temporary, fast-access storage area, known as a cache. This allows applications to access data more swiftly compared to fetching it from primary storage locations like databases or external storage systems.

Types of Caching

1. **In-Memory Caching**: This type of caching stores data in the server's RAM where the application is running, providing ultra-fast data access. However, it is volatile and data can be lost if the server is restarted.

2. **Distributed Caching**: Ideal for multi-server configurations, this method uses an external cache accessible by multiple applications or servers. Tools like

Redis and Memcached exemplify distributed caching, facilitating rapid data retrieval across a network.

3. **Database Caching**: Utilized internally by many databases, this automatically caches the results of frequently executed queries to enhance read performance without additional coding.

4. **Web Caching**: This occurs at various levels within a web architecture, including the use of CDNs (Content Delivery Networks) which cache content in multiple locations to reduce latency by serving data from geographically closer nodes to users.

Strategic Approaches to Caching

Implementing effective caching strategies is crucial for optimizing performance. Some prevalent strategies include:

1. **Cache-Aside**: Known as lazy loading, this strategy loads data into the cache only when necessary. If data is not found in the cache, it is retrieved from the primary store, cached, and then served.

```
public object GetData(string key)
{
    var data = cache.Get(key);
    if (data == null)
    {
        data = database.Fetch(key);
        cache.Set(key, data);
    }
    return data;
}
```

2. **Read-Through**: Similar to cache-aside, but here the cache itself is responsible for fetching and storing the data when a cache miss occurs.

3. **Write-Through**: This involves synchronizing data writes to both the cache and the database to maintain consistency but may introduce a slight delay due to double write operations.

```
public void SaveData(string key, object data)
{
    database.Save(key, data);
    cache.Set(key, data);
}
```

4. **Write-Behind (Write-Back)**: Data is written first to the cache and then asynchronously to the database. This strategy decreases latency but risks data loss if the cache fails before the data is persisted.

5. **Time to Live (TTL)**: Assigns a lifespan to cached data. Once expired, the data is purged from the cache and will be fetched from the primary storage upon next access.

Caching Best Practices

- **Consistency**: It is crucial to keep the cache and the primary data store synchronized to prevent data staleness.

- **Cache Invalidation**: Effective strategies are needed to refresh or purge cached data when modifications occur.

- **Monitoring**: Continuous monitoring of cache performance and usage patterns helps optimize the caching strategy and troubleshoot potential issues.

- **Security**: Especially when caching sensitive information, ensure data is encrypted and access is controlled.

Conclusion

Caching is a highly effective tool in software optimization, crucial for boosting application responsiveness and scalability. By selecting and implementing the right caching strategies and adhering to best practices, developers can dramatically improve application performance. Whether leveraging in-memory caches for their speed, utilizing distributed caches to enhance scalability, or employing advanced strategies like write-behind for operational efficiency, caching can be customized to suit specific application needs and environments.

Asynchronous programming

Asynchronous programming is a critical methodology in software development that optimizes application performance and user experience. It facilitates concurrent task execution, allowing applications to handle background operations while maintaining responsiveness to user interactions. This approach is particularly beneficial in operations that traditionally require substantial wait times, such as data retrieval, file processing, or any network-related tasks.

Core Concepts of Asynchronous Programming

At its foundation, asynchronous programming involves detaching the timing of operations from the main flow of an application. This model contrasts sharply with synchronous programming, where tasks are executed in a sequential order, often leading to inefficiencies when the system waits for each task to complete before starting the next.

Benefits of Asynchronous Programming

The implementation of asynchronous programming offers several notable advantages:

1. **Enhanced Responsiveness**: Applications can continue to interact with users or perform other critical operations while background tasks are processed, thus preventing interface freezes or slowdowns.

2. **Optimal Resource Use**: This programming style allows for more efficient use of computational resources by reducing downtime and idle periods typically associated with synchronous operations.

3. **Concurrent Operations Management**: Asynchronous programming simplifies the management of tasks that can run concurrently, leveraging modern tools and frameworks that ease the complexity of handling parallel operations.

Challenges of Asynchronous Programming

However, asynchronous programming can introduce certain challenges:

1. **Increased Complexity**: Asynchronous code can be more complex to manage and debug due to its non-linear nature, which can complicate tracking the application state across different execution phases.

2. **Resource Starvation Risks**: Improper management of asynchronous tasks can lead to resource starvation, where too many operations overwhelm the system's ability to handle them effectively.

3. **Error Handling Complications**: Asynchronous operations can produce errors that are difficult to track and manage because they may not manifest until after the initial operation is considered complete.

Implementing Asynchronous Programming in C#

C#, among other modern programming languages, supports asynchronous programming through specific keywords and libraries designed to facilitate this approach:

```csharp
public async Task<string> RetrieveWebData(string url)
{
    using (HttpClient client = new HttpClient())
    {
        string result = await client.GetStringAsync(url);
        return result; // Returns the web data as a string
    }
}
```

In the example above, the **GetStringAsync** method retrieves data asynchronously from a web URL. The await keyword pauses the **RetrieveWebData** function until **GetStringAsync** completes, thus freeing up the executing thread to handle other tasks.

Best Practices in Asynchronous Programming

For effective asynchronous programming, adherence to several best practices is recommended:

1. **Strategic Use**: Apply asynchronous methods for tasks that inherently involve delays, like I/O functions, to avoid adding unnecessary complexity to the codebase.

2. **Avoid Mixing Code Styles**: Mixing synchronous and asynchronous code can create performance bottlenecks and potential deadlocks. It is advisable to maintain consistency by fully adopting asynchronous methods where possible.

3. **Robust Exception Handling**: Ensure that exceptions are handled thoughtfully to prevent runtime errors from destabilizing the application.

4. **Leverage Existing Libraries**: Utilize established frameworks and libraries that support asynchronous programming to ensure that implementations are both robust and efficient.

Conclusion

Asynchronous programming is a powerful technique for building applications that are both performant and responsive, particularly suitable for handling operations with high latency. While it introduces a layer of complexity to application design, proper adherence to best practices and effective use of development tools can mitigate these challenges, allowing developers to harness the full potential of asynchronous programming to improve scalability and efficiency.

Performance profiling and tools

Performance profiling is a critical process in software development aimed at evaluating the runtime behavior of applications to identify inefficiencies and performance bottlenecks. By using sophisticated tools to monitor and measure specific performance metrics like CPU utilization, memory consumption, and execution timelines, developers can detect areas that need optimization and thus enhance overall software performance and user interaction.

Overview of Performance Profiling

Performance profiling is the methodical analysis of a software application's execution that helps reveal the performance characteristics of various code segments. This approach generates vital metrics that pinpoint problems affecting application speed and resource usage, which are essential for streamlining software functionality.

The Importance of Performance Profiling

1. **Bottleneck Detection**: Profiling pinpoints the most resource-intensive sections of the application, which are crucial for targeted optimization.

2. **Optimization of Resource Consumption**: It provides insights into how an application consumes

resources, aiding in making enhancements to boost efficiency and response times.

3. **Scalability Improvements**: Data from profiling enables optimizations that help the application manage larger loads more effectively, improving scalability.

4. **User Experience Enhancement**: Faster and more responsive applications, achieved through effective profiling and optimization, lead to greater user satisfaction and better overall software performance.

Profiler Types

1. **CPU Profilers**: These analyze the time spent by each function in using CPU resources to highlight areas of high computational demand.

2. **Memory Profilers**: These focus on tracking an application's memory usage, useful for identifying memory leaks and optimizing memory allocation.

3. **I/O Profilers**: Important for applications with significant input/output operations, helping to optimize interactions with file systems and databases.

4. **Network Profilers**: These are essential for applications dependent on network performance, analyzing the efficiency of network calls and responses.

Tools for Performance Profiling

Various profiling tools cater to different needs and platforms:

1. **VisualVM**: A versatile Java profiling tool that provides insights into CPU, memory usage, and garbage collection activities.

2. **New Relic**: A comprehensive tool that facilitates real-time monitoring and profiling, particularly useful in live production environments.

3. **Perf**: Utilized primarily in Linux systems, this tool helps analyze CPU performance and system events at a low level.

4. **JetBrains dotTrace and dotMemory**: These tools specialize in profiling .NET applications, offering detailed analysis on CPU and memory usage.

Example: Profiling a Java Application with VisualVM

Using VisualVM to profile a Java application involves several key steps:

1. **Installation and Setup**: Download and install VisualVM from its official website.

2. **Launching the Application**: Start the Java application you wish to profile.

3. **Connecting VisualVM**: Launch VisualVM, which should automatically detect running Java processes on your machine.

4. **Profiling Session**:
    - Navigate to the 'Profiler' tab.
    - Choose to profile CPU, memory, or both.
    - Start the profiling session to begin collecting data.

5. **Analyzing Data**:
    - VisualVM displays real-time data about CPU and memory usage.
    - Identify methods or processes that consume excessive resources.

```
public class PerformanceTest {
    public void inefficientMethod() {
        for (int i = 0; i < 1000000; i++) {
            String s = "Number: " + i; // Example of inefficient code due to
                repetitive string operations
        }
    }
}
```

6. **Code Optimization**: Refine or rewrite inefficient code based on the profiling results to improve performance.

Best Practices in Performance Profiling

- **Routine Profiling**: Integrate profiling into your regular development and maintenance cycles to keep performance at its peak.

- **Detailed Focus**: Start with a broad profiling scope to identify major issues, then drill down to specific areas for detailed analysis.

- **Realistic Testing Conditions**: Simulate real user interactions to ensure the profiling accurately reflects live usage scenarios.

- **Diverse Tooling**: Use a combination of profiling tools to capture a broad spectrum of performance data across different aspects of the application.

Conclusion

Performance profiling is indispensable for developing and maintaining high-performance applications. It not only helps in identifying and fixing performance issues but also plays a crucial role in ensuring the application scales effectively and remains responsive under different load conditions. By leveraging the right profiling tools and following best practices, developers can significantly improve the efficiency, scalability, and user experience of their applications.

Chapter Thirteen

Deploying ASP.NET Core Web APIs

Deployment options

Deployment is a fundamental phase in the software development lifecycle where software is introduced into a production setting and made available for end-user interaction. Recognizing the diversity of deployment methodologies is key to selecting an optimal approach that ensures effective and secure software delivery. These methodologies range from conventional on-premises setups to advanced cloud-based configurations.

Traditional Deployment: On-Premises

On-premises deployment involves installing software on physical servers located within the organization's own facility. This approach grants full control over the hardware and software environments but necessitates significant investment in infrastructure and ongoing operational expenses.

Advantages:

- **Complete Control**: Full governance over the computing environment and data.

- **Enhanced Security**: Data remains within the company's physical and cyber perimeters.

- **High Customizability**: Ability to tailor both hardware and software to precise organizational needs.

Disadvantages:

- **Substantial Costs**: Requires significant capital for infrastructure and skilled personnel.

- **Scalability Challenges**: Physical constraints limit quick scalability; more resources mean more hardware.

- **Intensive Maintenance**: Demands consistent manual updates and system maintenance.

Cloud-Based Deployment

This method utilizes online-hosted resources to deploy applications, minimizing the dependency on physical infrastructure. There are several forms of cloud deployments:

1. **Public Cloud**: Managed by external providers like AWS, Azure, or Google Cloud, these services manage hardware off-site and offer scalable options.

2. **Private Cloud**: Provides many of the benefits of a public cloud but within a private network, offering greater control and security.

3. **Hybrid Cloud**: Integrates public and private cloud elements, facilitating flexible data and application management across environments.

Advantages:

- **Easy Scalability**: Allows for quick adjustments in service capacity without physical infrastructure changes.

- **Cost-Effectiveness**: Generally more affordable upfront, operating on usage-based payment models.

- **Reliable Uptime**: Cloud providers generally offer strong managed services with reliable uptime.

Disadvantages:

- **Limited Control**: Less control over the physical hosting infrastructure.

- **Internet Reliance**: Constant internet connectivity is essential.

- **Potential Security Risks**: External data storage can pose security risks, especially for sensitive information.

Containerization and Orchestration

Containerization encapsulates an application with all its dependencies into a container that can run consistently across any computing environment. Docker is a popular containerization platform.

Orchestration, using systems like Kubernetes, automates the scaling, deployment, and operational tasks of these containers.

Advantages:

- **High Portability**: Containers can be deployed on any system without compatibility issues.

- **Efficient Resource Use**: Containers are lightweight and utilize system resources more efficiently than traditional virtual machines.

- **Quick Deployment**: Facilitates fast deployment and management of container instances.

Disadvantages:

- **Operational Complexity**: Managing containers requires specialized skills and tools.

- **Resource Intensive**: High numbers of containers can consume significant system resources.

Serverless Computing

Serverless computing abstracts server management away, allowing developers to focus on coding. This model automates server provisioning and scaling, with costs based on the precise amount of resources consumed by applications.

Advantages:

- **Maintenance Reduction**: No server management needed, simplifying operations.

- **Cost Reduction**: You only pay for the resources your applications consume.

- **Deployment Ease**: Quick deployment capabilities, focusing solely on code.

Disadvantages:

- **Vendor Dependence**: Creates a reliance on specific cloud providers and their technologies.

- **Startup Delays**: Potential for initial latency due to cold starts in function activation.

- **Complex State Management**: Challenges in managing state across stateless function executions.

Choosing a Deployment Strategy

The choice of a deployment strategy should be influenced by several factors, including the regulatory environment, the nature of the application, scalability needs, and budget constraints. Considerations include:

- **Regulatory Compliance**: Certain sectors have strict data handling requirements which might dictate on-premises deployments.

- **Traffic Expectations**: Applications expecting variable or high traffic might benefit from cloud-based or containerized environments.

- **Budget Limitations**: Organizations with strict budgetary constraints might opt for cloud solutions or serverless computing to mitigate upfront expenditures.

Understanding these various deployment options helps organizations align their software delivery strategies with their operational goals and technical requirements. This strategic alignment is crucial for optimizing both the performance and the scalability of deployed applications.

Deploying to IIS

Deploying applications to Internet Information Services (IIS) is an essential skill for developers working within the Windows ecosystem. IIS serves as a robust platform for hosting web applications, supporting a wide range of internet protocols. This detailed guide explores the critical steps and best practices necessary for deploying applications effectively on IIS, from initial server setup to post-deployment optimization.

Key Considerations for IIS Deployment

Deploying to IIS requires careful planning both in terms of software preparation and server configuration. This process involves setting up the server environment, configuring IIS correctly, uploading the application, and fine-tuning the deployment for optimal performance and security.

Preparation Before Deployment

Ensuring the server and environment are ready before deploying an application to IIS is crucial:

1. **Server Setup**: Make sure the Windows Server is updated and has IIS installed. This is typically done through the Server Manager, where the Web Server (IIS) role can be added along with required features like .NET support.

2. **Application Pool Setup**: Create and configure an application pool in IIS, which will isolate your application from others on the server, using its dedicated process environment. It's crucial to set the correct .NET CLR version and manage settings like maximum memory usage.

3. **Security Configurations**: Configure necessary security settings to protect your application. This includes setting up authentication methods,

authorization rules, and securing sensitive data like connection strings.

4. **Database Access**: Ensure the server has the correct permissions to access the database that your application will interact with.

5. **Resolve External Dependencies**: Confirm that all external services and APIs your application relies on are accessible from the server.

Steps to Deploy an Application on IIS

The deployment process includes several key actions:

1. **Publish the Application**: First, publish your application from Visual Studio or another integrated development environment. This compiles the application and creates a deployment package.

```
<PropertyGroup>
    <PublishProtocol>FileSystem</PublishProtocol>
    <PublishSiteName>MySite</PublishSiteName>
    <PublishDir>\\path\to\deployment\location\</PublishDir>
    <DeleteExistingFiles>True</DeleteExistingFiles>
</PropertyGroup>
```

2. **Transfer Files**: Move the deployment package to the IIS server, using methods like FTP, network shares, or direct file copy.

3. **Set Up IIS**: In IIS Manager, set up a new site or configure an existing one to host the application. Direct the site's root folder to where the deployment files are located.

- Configure site bindings to include IP address, port, and host name.
- Link the site to its designated application pool.

4. **Launch and Test**: After deployment, access the application via a browser to ensure it functions correctly. Check both application and IIS logs for any errors or potential issues that might need resolving.

Post-Deployment Optimization

After deploying an application, consider these steps to maintain and enhance its performance and security:

1. **Monitor and Tune Performance**: Use tools like IIS logs and Windows Performance Monitor to track performance. Adjust settings such as application pool recycling to manage resources better.

2. **Stay Updated**: Regularly update IIS and the Windows Server to protect against vulnerabilities. Use features like firewalls, and IIS security enhancements to prevent unauthorized access.

3. **Implement Backups**: Regularly back up your application data and IIS configurations to recover quickly from data loss or corruption.

4. **Plan for Scalability**: If application demand grows, consider strategies such as load balancing or upgrading server hardware to accommodate increased traffic.

Effective deployment to IIS not only involves technical preparation and execution but also requires ongoing management to ensure that the application remains secure, performant, and scalable. By adhering to these guidelines, developers and system administrators can ensure a successful deployment on IIS, providing a stable and efficient environment for web applications.

Deploying to Azure

Deploying applications on Microsoft Azure harnesses the capabilities of one of the leading cloud computing platforms, offering scalability, adaptability, and efficient management. Azure facilitates diverse deployment scenarios, from traditional computing environments and web services to modern container orchestration and serverless architectures. Understanding Azure's extensive deployment services is key to leveraging this platform for efficient application delivery.

Azure Deployment Frameworks

Azure provides several deployment options tailored to various needs, from comprehensive virtual environments to lightweight, flexible services:

1. **Azure Virtual Machines (VMs)**: Suitable for applications requiring traditional server environments, these virtual machines offer extensive control over a cloud-based virtual server.

2. **Azure App Services**: This managed platform is ideal for hosting web applications, supporting multiple programming languages and frameworks, allowing for easy scaling and management.

3. **Azure Kubernetes Service (AKS)**: For applications that utilize containers, AKS offers robust Kubernetes management, simplifying deployment and scalability of containerized applications.

4. **Azure Functions**: This serverless framework allows developers to run code in response to events, focusing on code execution without the overhead of server management.

Pre-Deployment Strategies

Effective deployment on Azure requires careful preparation:

- **Architectural Design**: Select the most suitable Azure deployment model based on application requirements and scalability needs.

- **Resource Management**: Organize all related Azure resources within a resource group for streamlined management and consolidated billing.

- **Security Compliance**: Implement Azure's security tools and protocols to ensure your deployment adheres to required security standards and compliances.

Deploying on Azure Virtual Machines

Deploying an application to an Azure VM involves several stages:

1. **Setting up the VM**: Configure a virtual machine using Azure's portal, CLI, or PowerShell, specifying the operating system and machine specifications.

```
az vm create --resource-group myResourceGroup --name myVM --image UbuntuLTS
   --generate-ssh-keys
```

2. **Configuring Network Settings**: Establish appropriate network settings and security measures to ensure safe and restricted access to the VM.

3. **Installing the Application**: Deploy your application onto the VM using similar methods as you would on a local machine.

Deploying on Azure App Services

Azure App Services makes web application deployment effortless:

1. **Establishing an App Service Plan**: Set up your plan with the required performance specifications.

```
az appservice plan create --name myAppServicePlan --resource-group myResourceGroup
   --sku S1
```

2. **Application Deployment**: Utilize Azure's deployment mechanisms like Git, FTP, or CI/CD integrations such as Azure DevOps to deploy and manage your application seamlessly.

Deploying on Azure Kubernetes Service (AKS)

AKS caters to containerized applications, facilitating their management and deployment:

1. **Creating an AKS Cluster**: Configure the Kubernetes cluster to suit your operational requirements.

```
az aks create --resource-group myResourceGroup --name myAKSCluster --node-count 3
--enable-addons monitoring --generate-ssh-keys
```

2. **Container Deployment**: Use Kubernetes commands or configuration files to manage and scale your containerized applications effectively.

Deploying on Azure Functions

For serverless application deployment, Azure Functions provides an efficient and straightforward approach:

1. **Setting Up a Function App**: Create a function app within your Azure resource group to act as a host for your functions.

```
az functionapp create --resource-group myResourceGroup --consumption-plan-location
westus --runtime python --name myFunctionApp --storage-account
mystorageaccount
```

2. **Deploying Code**: Implement your functions by uploading the code through the Azure portal, CLI, or via CI/CD pipelines for continuous updates.

Best Practices for Azure Deployment

- **Deployment Automation**: Leverage Azure CLI scripts or establish CI/CD pipelines for consistent and error-free deployments.

- **Ongoing Monitoring**: Use Azure Monitor and Application Insights to keep tabs on application performance and tweak configurations as needed.

- **Security Updates**: Regularly update your security settings to align with Azure's security enhancements and compliance updates.

Conclusion

Deploying to Azure provides a vast range of services tailored to meet different application needs, from managing heavy-duty virtual machines to facilitating agile serverless functions. By strategically choosing suitable services and adhering to deployment best practices, organizations can fully exploit Azure's potential to boost application performance and operational efficiency.

Ensuring security in production

Maintaining robust security in production environments is crucial for protecting applications and data against the evolving landscape of cyber threats. Establishing effective security measures ensures the integrity, availability, and confidentiality of critical resources, reinforcing trust with users and stakeholders.

Comprehensive Security Landscape

Effective production security involves multiple layers—from safeguarding physical infrastructure to implementing advanced network protections and enhancing application security.

Physical and Network Security Measures

1. **Physical Security**: Implement strict access controls to data centers and server rooms, utilizing biometric scans, surveillance systems, and secure access protocols to prevent unauthorized physical access.

2. **Network Security**: Deploy advanced firewall configurations, intrusion detection systems (IDS), and intrusion prevention systems (IPS) to secure network traffic. Employing network segmentation and Virtual Private Networks (VPNs) further helps in reducing the risk of data breaches within the network.

```
# Example command to block inbound traffic on a specific port using iptables
iptables -A INPUT -p tcp --dport 22 -j DROP
```

Enhancing Application Security

Robust application security measures are essential for minimizing vulnerabilities:

1. **Code Review and Static Analysis**: Regularly review the code for potential security issues and utilize Static Application Security Testing (SAST) tools to automate these checks.

2. **Dynamic Application Testing**: Implement Dynamic Application Security Testing (DAST) to identify vulnerabilities in running applications by simulating cyber attacks.

3. **Dependency Management**: Ensure all third-party libraries and dependencies are regularly updated and

secure. Tools like OWASP Dependency Check can help identify and mitigate known vulnerabilities.

```
# Command to initiate a scan for vulnerable dependencies
dependency-check --project "My Project" --scan ./path-to-project
```

Data Encryption and Key Management

Effective data protection strategies include:

1. **Data Encryption**: Implement robust encryption protocols such as AES-256 for encrypting data at rest and TLS 1.3 for securing data in transit.

2. **Key Management**: Utilize secure key management systems like AWS KMS or Azure Key Vault to manage and safeguard cryptographic keys.

```
# Command to create a Key Vault in Azure for managing cryptographic keys
az keyvault create --name "MyKeyVault" --resource-group "MyResourceGroup" --location "eastus"
```

Identity and Access Management (IAM)

Implementing strong IAM practices is critical for effective access control:

1. **Multi-factor Authentication (MFA)**: Ensure MFA is enforced to provide an additional layer of security beyond just passwords.

2. **Role-Based Access Control (RBAC)**: Implement RBAC to ensure users and systems have only the necessary permissions required to perform their roles.

3. **Access Audits**: Regularly perform audits of user activities and permissions to ensure compliance with security policies and to detect any anomalous behavior.

Security Monitoring and Incident Response

Ongoing monitoring and a robust incident response strategy are vital for early detection and management of security incidents:

1. **Continuous Monitoring**: Utilize Security Information and Event Management (SIEM) systems to monitor security events in real-time. Configuring tools like Splunk or the ELK Stack provides insights into security logs and helps in detecting anomalies.

2. **Incident Response Plan**: Maintain an updated incident response plan that clearly defines roles, responsibilities, and procedures for addressing security incidents.

```
# Example setup for monitoring suspicious login attempts
monitor {
  source: "/var/log/auth.log"
  match: "Failed password for"
  alert: "High"
}
```

Regulatory Compliance and Security Best Practices

Staying compliant with regulatory requirements and adopting security best practices is crucial:

1. **Maintaining Standards Compliance**: Strive to achieve and retain compliance with standards like

GDPR, HIPAA, or PCI-DSS, which are critical for operational and legal security assurance.

2. **Following Best Practices**: Align with security recommendations and frameworks from recognized bodies such as NIST or the Center for Internet Security (CIS) to ensure comprehensive security measures.

Conclusion

Securing production environments demands a layered and proactive approach, from physical security measures to sophisticated application and data security strategies. By embracing a comprehensive security strategy, including regular updates, stringent access controls, and proactive monitoring, organizations can effectively shield their assets from contemporary cyber threats, thereby bolstering their operational security posture and maintaining robust stakeholder confidence.

Conclusion

Recap of what has been learned

Reflecting on acquired knowledge and skills in technology and project management is crucial for solidifying understanding and identifying areas for future growth. This recap provides an overview of the key learnings across various aspects of technology, emphasizing the integration of theoretical concepts with practical execution.

Fundamental Concepts and Application

1. Integration of Theory and Practice: A strong grasp of foundational theories is essential for their effective application in real-world scenarios. For instance, understanding and implementing Object-Oriented Programming (OOP) concepts such as encapsulation, inheritance, and polymorphism significantly impact the quality and maintainability of software projects.

Code Example:

```java
// Java example demonstrating polymorphism
public class Animal {
    public void sound() {
        System.out.println("Animal makes a sound");
    }
}

public class Dog extends Animal {
    @Override
    public void sound() {
        System.out.println("Dog barks");
    }
}

public static void main(String[] args) {
    Animal myAnimal = new Dog();
    myAnimal.sound();  // Outputs: Dog barks
}
```

2. Project Management Approaches: Learning and applying various project management methodologies like Agile, Scrum, and Kanban have been pivotal in managing projects more effectively, emphasizing adaptability, iterative learning, and collaborative success.

3. Advanced Technology Skills: Engagement with state-of-the-art technologies such as machine learning, cloud computing (AWS, Azure), and contemporary web frameworks (React, Angular) has expanded technical skills and adaptability.

Sample Code Snippet:

```python
# Python example for a basic machine learning model using scikit-learn
from sklearn.ensemble import RandomForestClassifier
from sklearn.datasets import load_iris

# Load and prepare data
data = load_iris()
X, y = data.data, data.target

# Model training
model = RandomForestClassifier()
model.fit(X, y)

# Making predictions
predictions = model.predict(X)
```

Skill Development

1. Analytical and Problem-Solving Abilities: Addressing complex issues has enhanced analytical and problem-solving capabilities, enabling more efficient and effective resolution of challenges.

2. Communication and Team Collaboration: Experience in projects has bolstered communication skills, vital for articulating ideas and facilitating team interaction using tools like Slack, JIRA, and Git.

3. Continuous Learning and Flexibility: The rapid pace of technological advancement necessitates continuous learning and the ability to quickly adapt to new tools and technologies.

Areas for Further Growth

While substantial progress has been made, certain areas are highlighted for further development:

1. Specialization in Specific Technologies: Deepening knowledge in specialized fields such as data science or cybersecurity could refine expertise and open new professional pathways.

2. Leadership and Strategic Insight: Enhancing capabilities in leadership and strategic project planning would provide a more holistic approach to managing larger initiatives.

3. Mastery of Complex System Implementations: Increasing hands-on experience with complex systems and architectures would better elucidate their challenges and management strategies.

Conclusion

This recap not only reinforces the knowledge and skills gained but also sets the stage for continued professional development. By building on existing knowledge and strategically addressing areas of improvement, there is a clear path forward for further growth and significant contributions to the technology field.

How to continue growing as an ASP.NET Core developer

To continue evolving as an ASP.NET Core developer, one must embrace continual education, stay aligned with technological advancements, and refine application development skills. ASP.NET Core is a robust framework for creating high-performance web applications across various platforms such as Windows, Linux, and macOS. Keeping up-to-date with the framework's progress and enhancing your capabilities are essential for sustained professional growth in this field.

1. Deepen Your Understanding of Core Concepts

Strengthen Foundation Knowledge: Focus on fully grasping the fundamental aspects of ASP.NET Core, such as MVC architecture, dependency injection, middleware, and endpoint routing. These principles are crucial for adapting to changes within the framework and enhancing your development practices.

```
public void ConfigureServices(IServiceCollection services)
{
    services.AddControllersWithViews();
}
```

Venture into Complex Features: Advance to exploring more intricate features like SignalR for real-time functionalities, Blazor for building interactive client-side UIs with C#, and managing background tasks efficiently in ASP.NET Core.

2. Keep Current with Industry Changes

Stay Informed on Framework Updates: Regularly check for updates, enhancements, and new releases in ASP.NET Core. Microsoft's official ASP.NET Blog is a valuable resource for the latest developments, tutorials, and community features.

Participate in Developer Communities: Engage actively in community discussions, attend developer webinars, and participate in meetups (either virtual or local). These interactions can provide valuable insights and networking opportunities that propel your career forward.

3. Adhere to Best Practices

Uphold High Standards in Coding: Follow established coding standards and best practices such as the SOLID principles and common design patterns, which help in maintaining high-quality code that is scalable and efficient.

Prioritize Security Measures: Focus on mastering secure coding practices, particularly in authentication, authorization, and secure data handling within ASP.NET Core, leveraging ASP.NET Core Identity, and implementing secure APIs with OAuth.

```
services.AddAuthentication(options =>
{
    options.DefaultAuthenticateScheme = JwtBearerDefaults.AuthenticationScheme;
    options.DefaultChallengeScheme = JwtBearerDefaults.AuthenticationScheme;
});
```

4. Engage in Hands-On Projects

Develop Personal Projects: Use personal projects as a platform to apply theoretical knowledge practically, ranging from simple applications to complex systems that integrate various services and APIs.

Contribute to Open Source: Participate in open-source projects that utilize ASP.NET Core, which can help sharpen your coding skills and enhance your professional reputation.

5. Expand Your Skill Set

Master Front-End Technologies: Learn and master complementary front-end technologies such as JavaScript, Angular, React, or Vue.js, as full-stack development capabilities are increasingly beneficial.

Embrace Cloud Technologies: Skill up on deploying and operating ASP.NET Core applications within cloud environments like Azure or AWS, integrating with cloud services to maximize the functionality and scalability of your applications.

```
public static void Main(string[] args)
{
    CreateHostBuilder(args).Build().Run();
}

public static IHostBuilder CreateHostBuilder(string[] args) =>
    Host.CreateDefaultBuilder(args)
        .ConfigureWebHostDefaults(webBuilder =>
        {
            webBuilder.UseStartup<Startup>();
        });
```

6. Continue Your Formal Education

Pursue Certifications: Consider obtaining certifications like the Microsoft Certified: Azure Developer Associate, which can both credentialize your skills and deepen your technical understanding.

Broaden Your Knowledge Through Reading: Regularly consume literature on the latest trends in ASP.NET Core, software architecture, and technology innovations to keep your skills sharp and informed.

Conclusion

Advancing as an ASP.NET Core developer is a journey of continuous learning and application. By deepening your understanding of both foundational and advanced aspects, keeping pace with new developments, and applying your knowledge in practical settings, you can effectively enhance your expertise and propel your career forward in the ever-evolving landscape of web development.

Further resources and communities

For ASP.NET Core developers keen on enhancing their expertise and expanding their professional networks, the internet is a treasure trove of resources and community platforms. Actively engaging with these can significantly boost a developer's skill set and open doors to new opportunities within the rapidly evolving tech industry. Below is a guide to some essential resources and communities that are instrumental for developers pursuing growth in ASP.NET Core and beyond.

1. Educational Resources

Pluralsight

- **Overview**: Known for its comprehensive library, Pluralsight offers extensive courses on ASP.NET Core designed by industry experts.
- **Features**: Features learning paths, skills assessments, and course suggestions tailored to your progress.

- **Website**: Pluralsight

Udemy

- **Overview**: Provides a plethora of ASP.NET Core courses tailored to various skill levels, from beginner to advanced.

- **Features**: Offers courses at affordable prices, often available at significant discounts, with permanent access.

- **Website**: Udemy

LinkedIn Learning

- **Overview**: Hosts a broad range of tutorials and courses on ASP.NET Core, suitable for boosting professional skills.

- **Features**: Allows users to add completed courses to their LinkedIn profiles, showcasing their credentials.

- **Website**: LinkedIn Learning

2. Community Forums and Interactive Platforms

Stack Overflow

- **Overview**: An essential tool for developers seeking quick fixes to coding issues or looking to assist others in the ASP.NET Core community.

- **Features**: A vast reservoir of user-generated content with options for community interaction and technical discussion.

- **Website**: Stack Overflow

GitHub

- **Overview**: A hub for coding collaboration, GitHub is essential for managing, sharing, and reviewing code.
- **Features**: Provides a platform to contribute to open-source projects and collaborate with developers worldwide.
- **Website**: GitHub

3. Technology Blogs and Regular Updates

Scott Hanselman's Blog

- **Overview**: Offers insights and practical tips from one of the .NET community's most respected figures.
- **Features**: Contains a mix of technical tutorials and reflections on broader technology trends.
- **Website**: Scott Hanselman's Blog

ASP.NET Community Standup

- **Overview**: A weekly video broadcast by the ASP.NET team, showcasing the latest updates and community projects.
- **Features**: Provides an opportunity for live interaction with the ASP.NET Core team, enhancing community engagement.
- **Website**: ASP.NET Community Standup

4. Professional Networking via Meetups and Conferences

Meetup.com

- **Overview**: Connects users with local and virtual meetups focusing on ASP.NET Core and other technologies.
- **Features**: Excellent for fostering personal connections, knowledge exchange, and professional networking.
- **Website**: Meetup

Tech Conferences

- **Overview**: Attending conferences like Microsoft Ignite and .NET Conf is invaluable for immersion in the latest industry developments.
- **Features**: Participants can engage in workshops, absorb keynotes, and network with fellow tech professionals.
- **Websites**: Microsoft Ignite, NET Conf

5. Social Media Engagement

LinkedIn Groups

- **Overview**: ASP.NET developers can find specialized groups on LinkedIn for sharing information, networking, and engaging in discussions.
- **Features**: Enhances visibility and connectivity within the tech community, facilitating career development.

- **Website**: LinkedIn

Twitter

- **Overview**: Keeping up with prominent developers and community leaders on Twitter provides insights into the latest ASP.NET Core trends.

- **Features**: Instant access to industry news and expert opinions.

- **Example Profiles**: @shanselman, @davidfowl

Conclusion

Developing a career in ASP.NET Core involves more than just coding skills; it requires active participation in a broad ecosystem of learning platforms, community forums, tech blogs, professional networks, and social media. By engaging with these resources, developers not only stay updated with the latest technological advancements but also gain exposure to a wide array of professional opportunities, ensuring they remain at the forefront of the technology curve. This comprehensive approach is essential for anyone looking to excel and evolve within the dynamic field of technology.

Closing thoughts and encouragement

As we wrap up our discussion on the essential resources and strategies for ASP.NET Core developers, let's reflect on the broader journey of perpetual learning and career advancement in the tech sector. The technology field is inherently dynamic, with new advancements and tools continually reshaping the landscape. For developers immersed in the ASP.NET Core environment, staying updated and honing skills is not merely beneficial; it's essential.

Commit to Continuous Learning

The pursuit of knowledge in software development is never-ending. Innovations emerge rapidly, and today's new techniques quickly become tomorrow's standards. Platforms such as Pluralsight, Udemy, and LinkedIn Learning provide invaluable resources that help developers keep pace with current trends and deepen their understanding of complex topics through hands-on projects and comprehensive courses.

The Value of Community Involvement

Engaging with professional communities is crucial. Interaction within forums like Stack Overflow, contributions to open-source projects on GitHub, or attendance at industry conferences, each serves as a rich opportunity for learning and networking. These communities are vital for exchanging knowledge, sparking innovation, and even shaping the future direction of technologies.

The Importance of Practical Application

True mastery in ASP.NET Core comes from applying theoretical knowledge to real-world projects. Whether it's personal projects or community contributions, practical application cements concepts and highlights areas needing further exploration or refinement. It also significantly enhances a developer's portfolio, which is crucial for professional growth.

```csharp
// Simple example of implementing ASP.NET Core middleware
public class CustomMiddleware
{
    private readonly RequestDelegate _next;

    public CustomMiddleware(RequestDelegate next)
    {
        _next = next;
    }

    public async Task InvokeAsync(HttpContext context)
    {
        // Logic before the next middleware
        await context.Response.WriteAsync("Executing before ");

        await _next(context); // Proceeding to the next middleware

        // Logic after the next middleware
        await context.Response.WriteAsync(" and executing after");
    }
}

// Extension method to add the middleware to the HTTP request pipeline
public static class CustomMiddlewareExtensions
{
    public static IApplicationBuilder UseCustomMiddleware(this IApplicationBuilder builder)
    {
        return builder.UseMiddleware<CustomMiddleware>();
    }
}
```

Maintain Curiosity and Resilience

Curiosity is the engine of progress. It encourages developers to question, to explore, and to innovate. In a field where change is the only constant, maintaining an inquisitive spirit can lead to significant breakthroughs and solutions. Additionally, resilience in the face of setbacks—learning from failures and persisting through challenges—is a skill that distinguishes the successful.

Words of Encouragement

To all ASP.NET Core developers, remember that your journey is fraught with abundant learning opportunities, community support, and immense potential for personal and professional growth. The path may appear daunting due to the fast-paced nature of tech developments, but the rewards of steadfast learning and active engagement are profound. Embrace challenges, engage with the community, share your insights, and continuously seek knowledge. By doing so, you position yourself not just to succeed but to excel in the evolving tech landscape.

In closing, continue to learn, continue to code, and continue to challenge the confines of your capabilities with ASP.NET Core. Your potential is expansive, limited only by the extent of your engagement and curiosity.

www.ingramcontent.com/pod-product-compliance
Lightning Source LLC
Chambersburg PA
CBHW052146220526
45471CB00004B/1554